New Directions for
Child and Adolescent
Development

Reed W. Larson
Lene Arnett Jensen
EDITORS-IN-CHIEF

William Damon
FOUNDING EDITOR

Family Mealtime as a Context of Development and Socialization

Reed W. Larson
Angela R. Wiley
Kathryn R. Branscomb
EDITORS

Number 111 • Spring 2006
Jossey-Bass
San Francisco

FAMILY MEALTIME AS A CONTEXT OF DEVELOPMENT AND SOCIALIZATION
Reed W. Larson, Angela R. Wiley, Kathryn R. Branscomb (eds.)
New Directions for Child and Adolescent Development, no. 111
Reed W. Larson, Lene Arnett Jensen, Editors-in-Chief

© 2006 Wiley Periodicals, Inc., a Wiley company. All rights reserved.

No part of this publication may be reproduced, stored in a retrieval system, or transmitted in any form or by any means, electronic, mechanical, photocopying, recording, scanning, or otherwise, except as permitted under Section 107 or 108 of the 1976 United States Copyright Act, without either the prior written permission of the Publisher or authorization through payment of the appropriate per-copy fee to the Copyright Clearance Center, 222 Rosewood Drive, Danvers, MA 01923, (978) 750-8400, fax (978) 646-8600. Requests to the Publisher for permission should be addressed to the Permissions Department, John Wiley & Sons, Inc., 111 River Street, Hoboken, NJ 07030, (201) 748-6011, fax (201) 748-6008, www.wiley.com/go/permissions.

Microfilm copies of issues and articles are available in 16mm and 35mm, as well as microfiche in 105mm, through University Microfilms Inc., 300 North Zeeb Road, Ann Arbor, Michigan 48106-1346.

ISSN 1520-3247   electronic ISSN 1534-8687

NEW DIRECTIONS FOR CHILD AND ADOLESCENT DEVELOPMENT is part of The Jossey-Bass Education Series and is published quarterly by Wiley Subscription Services, Inc., a Wiley company, at Jossey-Bass, 989 Market Street, San Francisco, California 94103-1741. Periodicals postage paid at San Francisco, California, and at additional mailing offices. Postmaster: Send address changes to New Directions for Child and Adolescent Development, Jossey-Bass, 989 Market Street, San Francisco, CA 94103-1741.

New Directions for Child and Adolescent Development is indexed in PsycInfo, Biosciences Information Service, Current Index to Journals in Education (ERIC), Psychological Abstracts, and Sociological Abstracts.

SUBSCRIPTIONS cost $90.00 for individuals and $220.00 for institutions, agencies, and libraries.

EDITORIAL CORRESPONDENCE should be e-mailed to the editors-in-chief: Reed W. Larson (larsonr@uiuc.edu) and Lene Arnett Jensen (jensenl@cua.edu).

Jossey-Bass Web address: www.josseybass.com

CONTENTS

1

This introduction to the volume examines the evolution of contemporary family mealtime practices and how they have changed, and it synthesizes theory and research from across disciplines regarding the opportunities that mealtimes provide for child and adolescent development.

Forms and Functions of Family Mealtimes: Multidisciplinary Perspectives

Reed W. Larson, Kathryn R. Branscomb, Angela R. Wiley

For many families, mealtimes are the only time of the day when their members come together. These shared meals have come to symbolize family unity. In the United States, popular sources represent the mealtime as a foundational activity that has historically served vital functions, particularly in the socialization of children. But they also present family mealtimes as a practice that is threatened and diminishing in the rush of contemporary families' lives. Parenting articles advocate that "the family that eats together stays together" (Grant, 2001, para. 1) and warn parents that family mealtimes are "going the way of the dinosaur" (Garrett, 2000, para. 5).

This popular discourse poses important questions for critical scholarly evaluation. What elements of these widely shared beliefs are substantive reality, and what is cultural myth making? First, there is the historic question: Was there really a past era when families consistently gathered at the table for shared meals? And is the family mealtime really disappearing or just changing form? Then there is the question of functions. Are family meals all they are being cracked up to be? When families share meals as a

We express our strong appreciation to the Pampered Chef Family Resiliency Program at the University of Illinois in Urbana-Champaign and The Pampered Chef, Ltd. for their support for the preparation of this volume. We also thank Elizabeth Pleck, Kerry Kennedy Wynn, and Nickki Pearce for contributions to this work.

NEW DIRECTIONS FOR CHILD AND ADOLESCENT DEVELOPMENT, no. 111, Spring 2006 © Wiley Periodicals, Inc.
Published online in Wiley InterScience (www.interscience.wiley.com) • DOI: 10.1002/cad.151

regular practice, are there positive benefits for children and adolescents: for their socialization, mental health, and nutrition? Along the way to addressing these questions are issues of conceptualizing the processes that occur at family meals and recognizing the variety of forms mealtimes take across the diversity of contemporary families.

Fortunately scholars in different fields have been conducting research on these questions, though largely in disciplinary isolation. This volume brings the scholarship together in one place. In the following chapters, preeminent mealtime researchers from the fields of history, cultural anthropology, psycholinguistics, psychology, and nutrition critically review findings in each of their respective fields, with a primary focus on the United States. These authors examine the history of family mealtimes, describe contemporary mealtime practices, elucidate the differing transactional processes that occur, and evaluate findings on the outcomes associated with family meals for children and adolescents.

In this introductory chapter, we briefly summarize principal concepts and findings from these different disciplines, drawing on the work of these authors and others.

Conceptualizing Family Mealtimes

Family meals are "densely packed events," write Fiese, Foley, and Spagnola (Chapter Five, this volume): "Much has to happen in approximately twenty minutes: food needs to be served and consumed, roles assigned, past events reviewed, and plans made." Certainly the length, specific activities, and the meanings and synchronization of these activities differ substantially across families and cultural groups. But this recognition of mealtimes as a package of recurring meaning-laden activities, or "practices," is essential to their conceptualization. Family mealtimes are a crossroads of both people and interactional processes. They are an occasion—a fairly unique occasion in some families—of family members' engagement around an at least partly shared agenda.

In unpacking mealtimes, we find it easiest to start with behavior. Family meals involve a coordinated arc of activities: shopping or gathering food, meal preparation, a prayer in some families, eating, conversation, and cleaning up. Ochs and Shohet (Chapter Three, this volume) identify a Peruvian culture where silence is expected at family meals, but in most American families conversation flows. It may include catching up on the day's events, discussing news of the world, storytelling, solving problems, and family planning, as well as argument and conflict (Snow & Beals, Chapter Four, this volume). Indeed linguists and family psychologists have studied family mealtimes because they are an excellent place to observe family talk. How this behavior, including talk, is shaped by parents' and children's different roles is an important topic of analysis. For example, women historically have held major responsibility, not only for food preparation but for management of family interactions (Cinotto, Chapter Two, this volume; DeVault, 1991; Tolson et al., 1995), and cultural groups differ in whether children are expected to keep quiet or speak up (Ochs & Shohet, Chapter Three, this volume). Patterns of mealtime behavior, including whether a mealtime occurs at all, are also shaped by family history, parents' jobs, social class, and other societal and institutional processes.

Unpacking mealtimes further requires understanding the symbolic processes that are intertwined with and animate these behaviors. Through mealtime activities and conversation, family members often enact and reaffirm cultural meanings, as well as create new shared meanings. First, mealtimes are "vehicles for and end points of culture" (Ochs & Shohet, this volume). In depending on women to cook, eating specific foods, or conversing in a particular language, families reaffirm cultural identities, values, and ideals. In encouraging children to be quiet or speak up, for example, they may reinforce cultural notions of hierarchy and child deference, or the idea that children have equal status. What happens at mealtimes can also be vehicles and end points for family-specific values and meanings. In telling inside stories and jokes, doing things in a certain ritual way, or acting out family tensions, members create and reinforce a particular family identity (Fiese et al., this volume).

Scholars often characterize family mealtimes as an activity setting, opportunity space, or cultural site, terms emphasizing that they are not fixed scripts but rather provide a structure of opportunities. Certainly family members come to the table with cultural and handed-down expectations: norms, values, feelings about what "needs" to occur. Yet they make choices and are creative within these givens: family members intentionally and unintentionally use them, build on them, or even challenge them. In a study of recent Bengali immigrants to the United States, Ray (2000) described how individual families drew on the two cultures, for example, in choosing to eat American breakfasts for convenience but following traditional Bengali dinner practices that reinforce their cultural identification. Similarly, Cinotto (this volume) describes "food fights" in Italian, Jewish, and Japanese immigrant families during the early 1900s in which family mealtimes were a site of confrontation and negotiation between generations. At the level of individual families, a parent may use the family meal as a regular opportunity to check up on a child's homework, or mealtimes may become an arena in which a son or daughter contests family power relationships through active resistance (Grieshaber, 1997).

Among the opportunities afforded by mealtimes are those for child development and socialization. Mealtimes provide special potential for fostering development, first, because they are a context in which children are a captive audience, at least for the few minutes it takes them to eat. In addition, mealtimes provide opportunities for parents to model, coach, monitor, and control children's behavior, as well as opportunities for children to be apprentices in meaningful activities. Furthermore, from the viewpoint of classical psychology, the innate enjoyment of eating potentially serves to reinforce and enliven children's other experiences at the meal table. And from a sociological perspective, the presence of multiple family members—a "reference group"—may contribute to children's perception that their families' mealtime practices represent normative reality.

Of course, just because opportunities exist does not mean they will be taken and realized. Families may differ greatly in their actual mealtime practices and how these practices influence young people. Before examining the functions of mealtimes for child socialization and development, it is important to understand the particular behaviors and meanings associated with mealtimes in the United States. What forms have mealtime practices taken and do they currently take?

Mealtime Forms: Past and Present

Most Americans think family mealtimes are a good idea. Over 80 percent of parents in one study viewed family dinners as important, and 79 percent of teens considered eating family meals to be among their top-rated family activities (Zollo, 1999). For many in the United States, the proper form for a family meal has been home-cooked food, planned and prepared most often by a woman, eaten at a regular time, according to prescribed etiquette regarding behaviors such as manners and assigned seating of family members (Cinotto, this volume). But do actual practices correspond to these values and traditional expectations? We begin with the historic question regarding past mealtime practices, and then examine whether mealtimes are disappearing and what forms they currently take.

The History of the American Family Mealtime. Was there a period in U.S. history when shared family meals were the norm? In this volume, the historian Simone Cinotto follows the development of family mealtimes in the United States from the 1850s through the 1950s. He reports that prior to the mid-nineteenth century, the family mealtime as we conceive it did not exist: "Early Americans of European descent felt free to eat wherever and whenever they could or wanted to in ways that resemble today's snacking." Although family members may often have eaten "in the same room at approximately the same time," many families did not have a table, only a couple of boards set on trestles, at which only the men were permitted to sit and eat. Gillis (1996) explains that agrarian families interacted with each other throughout the day, so the idea of mealtimes as a special occasion for family togetherness developed only as urbanization and industrialization made these other interactions less frequent.

The practice of a shared family meal emerged within the Victorian middle class in the late nineteenth century and was then adopted by upwardly mobile and immigrant families as a symbol of achieving middle-class status. The Victorian mealtime was a formal affair that served in part to reinforce status differentiations both between and within families (Gillis, 1996; Kasson, 1987). Cinotto reports that most poor white and African American families did not adopt the practice of family meals, because many women in these families worked away from home for long hours, their homes lacked a place for a shared meal, and other factors related to poverty. At the turn of the twentieth century, however, home economists, social workers, philanthropists, nutritionists, and others began a decades-long campaign to encourage family mealtimes, particularly in poor, working-class, and immigrant families. This large campaign was aimed at promoting mealtimes as an instrument of cultural assimilation, strengthening families, improving nutrition, and facilitating child development. But the Victorian family meal saw its widespread realization in the United States only during the postwar 1950s, when prosperity permitted the majority of the population to join the middle class (Bossard & Boll, 1950; Cinotto, this volume).

What history shows us, then, is that the family mealtime is a comparatively recent innovation in the United States, dating back only 150 years. And although we often think of mealtimes as a tradition, they were not practiced by a majority of families until the 1950s.

Current Mealtime Frequencies. What has happened to the American family mealtime since the 1950s? Is it being lost in the rush of modern life? Societal changes have created new obstacles to family meals, including women's increased rates of employment, more parents working nonstandard hours, longer commutes, and children's greater participation in extracurricular activities (Doherty, 2002; Neumark-Sztainer, Story, Ackard, Moe, & Perry, 2000). We look first at the frequency with which family meals currently occur and then at what forms they take.

Survey research suggests that a majority of children and adolescents eat dinner with their families on a regular basis. In the 2003 National Survey of Children's Health (NSCH), a nationally representative sample of 102,353 U.S. families was asked how often all resident family members ate together during the previous week. In families with children ages six to eleven, 80 percent reported a shared meal on four or more days, and 55 percent reported a shared meal on six or seven days. In families with twelve to eighteen year olds, 69 percent reported shared meals on four or more days, and 42 percent reported them on six or seven days (Child Trends, 2005). Estimates for adolescents were closely similar in another national survey of 18,177 youth in the seventh through twelfth grades (the Add Health Study): 69 percent of youth reported eating four or more evening meals with their families during the previous week, and 48 percent reported eating six or seven evening meals together (Videon & Manning, 2003). It is also worth noting that a biennial national survey of teens found that rates of family meals have remained stable since 1998 and may even have increased (CASA, 2005).

An important finding is that family mealtimes are frequent across demographic groups. Among the NSCH families with children six to eleven years old, shared meals were reported on four to seven days per week for 70 percent or more of households across ethnic groups, socioeconomic status (SES) levels, and family structure categories (Child Trends, 2005). Among families with eleven to eighteen year olds, shared meals were reported this often for 60 percent or more households across all of these same categories.

The NSCH data do show differences among demographic groups, particularly in rates of daily family meals (six to seven days per week). Only small variations were found by family structure and child's gender. But children and adolescents in immigrant families were more likely to report daily family meals than those in native-born families. In addition, Hispanic families were found to be above the norm and African American families below the norm in rates for daily family meals. Separate data for Asian American families were not presented for the NSCH survey; however Neumark-Sztainer (Chapter Six, this volume) found their rates of family meals to be higher than other ethnic groups. Finally, although low-income families have historically been less likely to have shared family meals, the NSCH found *more* frequent rates of daily meals for lower-SES families. (This SES difference was not found in a representative sample of urban and suburban Minnesota teens; in fact, teens in the highest-SES group reported eating meals with their families most frequently [Neumark-Sztainer, this volume].) Despite these differences, the data suggest that the majority of children and adolescents across demographic groups eat with their families.

In sum, this evidence indicates that the family mealtime is not disappearing. Even in adolescence, over half of young people eat with their families on four or more days per week. As Gillis (1996) writes, "Today we tend to both exaggerate the frequency with which families ate together in the past and to underestimate the commitment to the family dinner in the present" (p. 94).

Current Mealtime Practices.   Knowing that children and adolescents regularly eat with their families, however, does not tell us what actually happens at family meals. Are they hurried affairs focused only on food consumption? How closely do they resemble the traditional model of a proper family meal? Existing evidence suggests that the nature of family meals has changed and that they have become more varied since the 1950s.

The changes involve multiple mealtime practices. Mothers continue to shoulder the major responsibility for mealtimes (Bird, 1999; Harnack, Story, Martinson, Neumark-Sztainer, & Stang, 1998), but families have take-out food or eat out more often than they did twenty-five years ago (Guthrie, Lin, & Frazao, 2002). The television is on at dinnertime in many families: 63 percent of eight to eighteen year olds in a recent national survey said the television is "usually" on during meals (Rideout, Roberts, & Foehr, 2005). Historical analyses suggest that mealtime interactions have become more casual, and the nineteenth-century emphasis on formal manners has been replaced by "unspoken, almost subconscious guidelines and constraints" (Visser, 1991, p. 341). Furthermore, accounts from observational research (Blum-Kulka, 1997; Ramey & Juliusson, 1998; Snow & Beals, this volume) suggest that family mealtime interactions are less hierarchical and more inclusive of children than in the Victorian parlor dinner.

Families also appear to be quite diverse in what happens at mealtimes. Neumark-Sztainer and colleagues (2000) found large variation among families in the regularity of family meals, the nutritional value of the food, rules around meals, and whether conflict occurs. Some differences are related to the distinct mealtime practices of ethnic groups. We were struck, for example, by Martini's finding (1996) that the mealtimes of Japanese American families were less structured and more relaxed, and involved less overt conflict than in Anglo families, differences that she attributed to their contrasting emphasis on family harmony versus individual expression. Recent waves of immigration have also brought diverse foods and mealtime practices (Gabaccia, 1998; Ray, 2004). Further differences in diet and mealtime practices have been described that are related to social class (DeVault, 1991; Videon & Manning, 2003) and family structure (Larson, 2001; Ramey & Juliusson, 1998).

What this evidence suggests is that while children still eat with their families much of the time, these mealtimes may be moving further away from the Victorian model. Less effort goes into food preparation, and meals may be less formal and hierarchical than in the past. They are also highly varied in form, reflecting the diversity of contemporary American families. These changes do not necessarily mean that family mealtimes are less likely to be contexts of child socialization. Indeed, Blum-Kulka (1997) argues that the changes in modern dinner practices have been driven in part by the desire to make them more suited to facilitating development. This brings us to the question of the functions of family mealtimes.

Functions for Children: Developmental Processes and Outcomes

The issue of whether family meals provide special opportunities for young people's socialization and development is a linchpin to much of the public discourse on family mealtimes. Do family meals themselves, or particular forms they take in some families, facilitate young people's social, cognitive, emotional, and nutritional development? Scholars have employed the research paradigms of diverse fields to begin addressing this issue. They have provided valuable descriptions and theoretical formulations of the specific transactional practices that occur at family mealtimes and are beginning to provide evidence on whether these practices are related to outcomes for young people. We summarize these practices and outcomes for four domains of development that have received the most attention from researchers and are the topics of the chapters in this volume.

Cultural Socialization. One of the principal outcomes one can expect from children's participation in mealtimes is socialization into their families' culture. In this volume, anthropologists Elinor Ochs and Merav Shohet bring together scholarship on the ways in which mealtimes provide a context for cultural socialization. Drawing on examples from numerous cultures, they elucidate how mealtime practices solicit children's attention and involvement in ways that can lead to their socialization. First, these practices situate children as observers and overhearers: children are witnesses to both the distinctive structure and content of mealtime practices in their cultural group (see also Snow & Beals, this volume). In some cases, information and meaning are communicated through irony, metaphor, or silence. Second, mealtimes position children as active participants in cultural practices. Mealtime activities "recruit" children into preferred ways of thinking, feeling, and acting. Young people may play roles in preparing the meal, saying prayers, and recounting their stories of the day within culturally prescribed expectations. Of course, children are not solely imitators of cultural practices and meanings; they may resist and transform them, as well as introduce new practices and meanings to other family members.

The socialization outcomes attributed to these transactions include those specific to mealtimes and to cultural membership more generally. Through observation and participation, youth may internalize table manners, modes of mealtime conversation, and ways of thinking about food. For example, a dominant message to children in the United States is that food is important for health, while Italian families communicate the pleasurable qualities of the meal (Ochs & Shohet, this volume). Youth's observation and participation in mealtimes also apprentices them more generally in the roles, ways of relating, tools, and moral values of their culture. For example, numerous scholars have described meal preparation and mealtime practices as a salient arena for girls' socialization into cultural gender norms (DeVault, 1991; Feiring & Lewis, 1987). What children learn may also lead to changes in that culture. Elias (1939) marshaled evidence that the development of table manners in sixteenth-century Europe contributed to sharp declines in crime rates. Although the quantitative research paradigms of other disciplines have not been applied to examining these complex symbolic processes (and would not do them justice), existing evidence suggests that children's participation in shared meals is an important means of cultural socialization.

Literacy and Academic Outcomes. Acquiring literacy might be seen as an important component of cultural socialization, and scholars have been concerned with how mealtime conversation influences children's development of language and school work. Developmental psycholinguists Catherine Snow and Diane Beals (this volume) review evidence that the types of conversation that occur at family meals may provide special opportunities for young children's literacy development. They find that mealtimes in many middle-class and low-income families include frequent occasions of "explanatory talk," often in the form of extended dialogues between children and adults in which parents' reasoning about objects, concepts, events, or conclusions is conveyed. For example, the concept of a driver's license may be explained or new vocabulary introduced. Mealtimes in many homes also include the telling or co-construction of narratives, which among other things can communicate social context norms and expose children to thought about future and hypothetical events and the language of planning. Snow and Beals show that parents play important roles not only in generating these complex forms of talk, but also in supporting children's participation in them (see also Ochs & Shohet, this volume).

But do the rich conversations that occur around the dinner table really influence children's literacy? Snow and Beals report longitudinal research that suggests this is the case. Families differ greatly in how much of these different forms of talk occur at family meals. They have found that preschoolers' degree of exposure to narrative and explanatory talk predicted their vocabulary and reading achievement in the elementary school years. Parents' use of rare words and their use of strategies to support children's learning were associated with better vocabulary and other literacy outcomes as children grew older (Beals, 1997; Snow & Beals, this volume). Snow and Beals's research has not extended into the adolescent years, but correlational studies have found that teens who eat family meals more frequently also have higher grade point averages (Eisenberg, Olson, Neumark-Sztainer, Story, & Bearinger, 2004; Tepper, 1999).

The most provocative finding in this research is evidence that family mealtimes may provide richer opportunities for vocabulary development than other contexts of family interaction, including reading books with children (Weizman & Snow, 2001). The extended and far-ranging discussions that occur during meals in some families introduced children to more varied and novel words, and this was found to correlate with later vocabulary scores. Although Snow and Beals are clear that we should not discourage parents from reading to their children, they show that mealtimes are contexts for special kinds of talk that appear to facilitate children's literacy.

Risk Behavior and Socioemotional Development. Social interaction at the dinner table may serve as an arena for the cultivation of young people's social-emotional development. At the most basic level, correlational research shows that children and adolescents who regularly eat meals with their families are less likely to engage in risk behaviors and manifest emotional problems (CASA, 2005; Compañ, Moreno, Ruiz, & Pascual, 2002; Hofferth & Sandberg, 2001). Using survey data from forty-seven hundred ethnically and socioeconomically diverse adolescents,

Eisenberg and associates (2004) found that teens, particularly girls, who ate meals with their families were less likely to use drugs and alcohol, have low self-esteem, experience depression, or engage in suicidal thoughts or attempts. The Achilles' heel to many studies is the possibility of reverse causality: one can easily imagine that youth who are troubled or engaged in risk behaviors may be exactly those who are most likely to avoid meals with their families. An important contribution of Eisenberg and colleagues' findings was that the relationships between mealtime frequency and the effects for most of these outcome variables, though diminished, remained significant even after controlling for adolescents' reports of family connectedness.

It is essential, however, to ask what ingredients of family mealtimes are related to positive socioemotional outcomes for youth. One suspects that a parent forcing a resistant child to gobble down a piece of pizza in the family's presence is not a formula for positive development. In their contribution to this volume, Barbara Fiese, Kimberly Foley, and Mary Spagnola describe observational research that examines which mealtime practices are most influential. Fiese's studies have zeroed in on differences between families in how they communicate, whether they carry out and adhere to tasks, and how much continuity there is in mealtime activities and meanings. Families differ greatly in these practices. The authors illustrate, for example, how a father in one family escalated a child's reluctance to eat turkey into an angry exchange, while in other families, parents used mealtimes as opportunities for coaching children on challenging life situations and monitoring children's activities away from home.

Research indicates that differences among families in these types of transactions may mediate children's emotional development. In families where there is more direct communication and planning around mealtimes and where family members perceive shared activities like meals to have more symbolic meaning, children are less likely to experience anxiety and related internalizing symptoms (Markson & Fiese, 2000; Fiese & Greene, 1993; Fiese et al., this volume). Fiese and colleagues also find that family members' expressions of concern about others' feelings during family meals is associated with children's experiencing a sense of belonging and trust. Positive experiences at family meals may also increase children's resiliency. In two retrospective interview studies, the children of alcoholic parents were less likely to have later become alcoholic if dinner rituals had been maintained in their families of origin (Bennett, Wolin, Reiss, & Teitlebaum, 1987; Fiese & Greene, 1993). Although most of this research is limited to cross-sectional and retrospective methods, these findings begin to suggest that the meaning and pattern of interpersonal transactions that children experience at dinner can facilitate their emotional development.

Nutrition. Food, of course, is the raison d'être of mealtimes, and it is important to ask how family mealtimes influence children's nutrition and eating patterns. This is especially important in the United States where many children's and adolescents' diets are poor, contributing to their development of lifetime eating habits and a national epidemic of obesity. Family mealtimes potentially provide an orderly environment in which children have the opportunity to witness, practice, and internalize healthy eating patterns. In Chapter Six on adolescents' nutrition, epidemiologist Dianne Neumark-Sztainer presents findings pertinent to this thesis.

Studies by Neumark-Sztainer's team and others have begun to confirm the relationship of family meals with children's and adolescents' dietary intake. Using large-scale samples that bridge social classes and ethnic groups, researchers show that older children and teens who eat a greater number of family meals each week have more nutritious diets (Gillman et al., 2000, Neumark-Sztainer, Hannan, Story, Croll, & Perry, 2003; Neumark-Sztainer, this volume; Videon & Manning, 2003). Greater frequency of family meals is associated with increased consumption of fruits, vegetables, vitamins, calcium, and other essential nutrients and with lower intake of fried foods and soft drinks. These associations remain significant with controls for family sociodemographic characteristics. In addition, Neumark-Sztainer (this volume) finds an independent association between teens' eating more family meals and having a lower likelihood of engaging in extreme weight control behaviors, such as use of laxatives and self-induced vomiting.

Research also suggests that specific practices during family mealtimes are related to children's nutrition. Neumark-Sztainer (this volume) found that in families where the mealtime atmosphere was positive, shared meals were a priority, and there were mealtime rules and structure, teens were less likely to engage in disordered eating and unhealthy dieting behaviors. Importantly, a number of these relationships were significant even with controls for global measures of the quality of family relationships. This suggests that family practices specific to mealtimes contributed to the development of healthy eating behaviors. Conversely, in families where the television was on during the mealtime and arguments were frequent, family members were found to consume less healthy foods (Boutelle, Birnbaum, Lytle, Murray, & Story, 2003; Coon, Goldberg, Rogers, & Tucker, 2001). Like other authors in the volume, Neumark-Sztainer urges caution about concluding from existing evidence that mealtime practices have a causal relationship with the outcome variables under consideration. Nonetheless, these findings provide preliminary evidence that is consistent with the thesis that mealtimes can provide a context for young people's development of healthier eating behaviors.

Conclusion

This research on functions reinforces the idea that family mealtimes provide opportunities for young people's socialization and development. Although some studies indicate that simply having a shared family meal may contribute to development, research and theory lead us to believe that it is the specific practices of a family's mealtime that are most important. Evidence suggests that family mealtimes are an opportunity for families to engage children in cultural activities and meanings and, in so doing, help them become socialized as members of that culture. The extended explanations and narratives that occur in many families' mealtimes appear to provide a special opportunity for children's development of literacy. Preliminary evidence suggests that when family members communicate directly and imbue mealtime activities with meaning, these practices contribute to youth's socioemotional development; and when family meals provide an orderly context and a positive atmosphere, adolescents develop healthier eating patterns. A key idea across the chapters in this volume is that parents and older family members are important to determining whether these opportunities are realized. They make valuable contributions by helping structure a family's mealtime practices, modeling behavior, and coaching children.

It should be cautioned that existing evidence does not by any means provide proof of the strong claims about the positive functions of mealtimes in popular discourse. Families differ greatly in what transpires at the dinner table, and media discussions tend to ignore the potential for meals to be contexts of chronic tension, transmission of maladaptive forms of interaction, and children's development of unhealthy eating habits. More rigorous controlled studies are needed that test mediating processes and examine how diverse cultural practices may provide conditions for children's development. Nonetheless, current theory and research are consistent with the idea of family mealtimes as a context that is rich in opportunities for socialization and development.

Importantly, this research on functions comes at a time when mealtime forms are in flux. Although rates of family meals appear to be somewhat lower than in the 1950s, shared meals continue to be highly valued; and the majority of young people, across ethnic groups and social classes, eat with their families on most nights. At the same time, however, mealtime practices are moving away from the traditional model of dinnertime as a formal affair, involving a home-cooked meal, prepared by a housewife, that reinforces etiquette and hierarchy. The typical family meal is now more likely to involve fast food and television, elements that are not associated with nutrition and other benefits that mealtimes might provide. Yet there is evidence that social interactions at mealtimes are less hierarchical and more inclusive of children in ways that potentially facilitate young people's development and family well-being. These latter historic changes, it might be argued, provide increased opportunity for families to include children in affirming the meanings and values of their cultural heritage and in learning to give words to the complex events of family life. They provide opportunities for young people to participate in interactions that reinforce belonging and resiliency and develop a pattern of enjoying healthy food in communion with significant others. The excellent chapters in this volume provide much fuller and more nuanced discussion of these issues.

References

Beals, D. E. (1997). Sources of support for learning words in conversation: Evidence from mealtimes. *Journal of Child Language, 24,* 673–694.

Bennett, L. A., Wolin, S. J., Reiss, D., & Teitlebaum, M. A. (1987). Couples at risk for transmission of alcoholism: Protective influences. *Family Process, 26,* 111–129.

Bird, C. E. (1999). Gender, household labor, and psychological distress: The impact of the amount and division of housework. *Journal of Health and Social Behavior, 40,* 32–45.

Blum-Kulka, S. (1997). *Dinner talk: Cultural patterns of sociability and socialization in family discourse.* Mahwah, NJ: Erlbaum.

Bossard, J.H.S., & Boll, E. S. (1950). *Ritual in family living.* Philadelphia: University of Pennsylvania Press.

Boutelle, K. N., Birnbaum, A. S., Lytle, L. A., Murray, D. M., & Story, M. (2001). Perceptions of family mealtime environment and adolescent mealtime behavior: Do adults and adolescents agree? *Journal of Nutrition Education, 33*(3), 128–133.

CASA (National Center on Addiction and Substance Abuse at Columbia University). (2005). The importance of family meals II. Retrieved October 22, 2005, from http://www.casacolumbia.org/Absolutenm/articlefiles/380–2005_family_dinners_ii_final.pdf.

Child Trends. (2005). Family meals. Child Trend data bank. Retrieved October 18, 2005, from www.childtrendsdatabank.org.

Compañ, E., Moreno, J., Ruiz, M. T., & Pascual, E. (2002). Doing things together: Adolescent health and family rituals. *Journal of Epidemiology and Community Health, 56,* 89–94.

Coon, K. A., Goldberg, J., Rogers, B. L., & Tucker, K. L. (2001). Relationships between use of television during meals and children's food consumption patterns. *Pediatrics, 107,* 167–176.

DeVault, M. L. (1991). Feeding the family: The social organization of caring as gendered work. Chicago: University of Chicago Press.

Doherty, W. J. (2002). *Putting family first: Successful strategies for reclaiming family life in a hurry-up world.* New York: Holt.

Eisenberg, M. E., Olson, R. E., Neumark-Sztainer, D., Story, M., & Bearinger, L. H. (2004). Correlations between family meals and psychosocial well-being among adolescents. *Archives of Pediatrics and Adolescent Medicine, 158,* 792–796.

Elias, N. (1939). *The civilizing process.* Oxford: Basil Blackwell.

Feiring, C., & Lewis, M. (1987). The ecology of some middle class families at dinner. *International Journal of Behavioral Development, 10,* 377–390.

Fiese, B. H., & Greene, K. (1993). Family rituals in alcoholic and nonalcoholic households: Relations to adolescent health symptomatology and problem drinking. *Family Relations: Journal of Applied Family and Child Studies, 42,* 187–192.

Gabaccia, D. R. (1998). We are what we eat: *Ethnic food and the making of Americans.* Cambridge, MA: Harvard University Press.

Garrett, L. (2000). Food and nutrition: Mealtime mania. Retrieved June 15, 2005, from http://www.todaysparent.com/toddler/foodnutrition/article.jsp?content=6527&page=1.

Gillis, J. R. (1996). *A world of their own making: Myth, ritual, and the quest for family values.* New York: Basic Books.

Gillman, M. W., Rifas-Shiman, S. L., Frazier, A. L., Rockett, H. R., Camargo, C. A. Jr., Field, A. E., Berkey, C. S., & Colditz, G. A. (2000). Family dinner and diet quality among older children and adolescents. *Archives of Family Medicine, 9,* 235–240.

Grant, T. R. (2001). The family that eats together stays together. Retrieved June 15, 2005, from http://four-fold.tripod.com/essays/familymeal.html.

Grieshaber, S. (1997). Mealtime rituals: Power and resistance in the construction of mealtime rules. *British Journal of Sociology, 48*(4), 649–666.

Guthrie, J. F., Lin, B., & Frazao, E. (2002). Role of food prepared away from home in the American diet, 1977–78 versus 1994–1996: Changes and consequences. *Journal of Nutrition Education and Behavior, 34,* 140–150.

Harnack, L., Story, M., Martinson, B., Neumark-Sztainer, D., & Stang, J. (1998). Guess who's cooking? The role of men in meal planning, shopping, and preparation in U.S. households. *Journal of the American Dietetic Association, 98,* 995–1000.

Hofferth, S. L., & Sandberg, J. F. (2001). How American children spend their time. *Journal of Marriage and the Family, 63*(2), 295–308.

Kasson, J. F. (1987). Rituals of dining: Table manners in Victorian America. In K. Grover (Ed.), *Dining in America, 1850–1900* (pp. 114–141). Amherst: University of Massachusetts Press.

Larson, R. (2001). Mothers' time in two-parent and one-parent families: The daily organization of work, time for oneself, and parenting of adolescents. In K. Daly (Ed.), *Minding the time in family experience: Emerging perspectives and issues* (pp. 85–109). Oxford: Elsevier Science.

Markson, S., & Fiese, B. H. (2000). Family rituals as a protective factor for children with asthma. *Journal of Pediatric Psychology, 25,* 471–479.

Martini, M. (1996). "What's new?" at the dinner table: Family dynamics during mealtimes in two cultural groups in Hawaii. *Early Development and Parenting, 5,* 23–34.

Neumark-Sztainer, D., Hannan, P. J., Story, M., Croll, J., & Perry, C. (2003). Family meal patterns: Associations with sociodemographic characteristics and improved dietary intake among adolescents. *Journal of the American Dietetic Association, 103,* 317–322.

Neumark-Sztainer, D., Story, M., Ackard, D., Moe, J., & Perry, C. (2000). The "family meal": Views of adolescents. *Journal of Nutrition Education, 32,* 329–334.

Ramey, S. L., & Juliusson, H. K. (1998). Family dynamics at dinner: A natural context for revealing basic family processes. In M. Lewis & C. Feiring (Eds.), *Families, risk, and competence* (pp. 31–52). Mahwah, NJ: Erlbaum.

Ray, K. (2004). *The migrant's table: Meals and memories in Bengali-American Households.* Philadelphia: Temple University Press.

Rideout, V., Roberts, D. F., & Foehr, U. G. (2005). *Generation M: Media in the lives of 8–18 year-olds.* Washington, DC: Henry J. Kaiser Family Foundation.

Tepper, R. L. (1999). Parental regulation and adolescent time-use decisions: Findings from the NLSY97. In R. T. Michael (Ed.), *Social awakening: Adolescent behavior as adulthood approaches* (pp. 77–103). New York: Russell Sage Foundation.

Tolson, T.F.J., Wilson, M. N., Hinton, I. D., Simmons, F., Staples, W., & Askew, T. (1995). An analysis of adult-child conversation patterns in diverse African American families. In M. N. Wilson (Ed.), *African American family life: Its structural and ecological aspects* (pp. 59–72). San Francisco: Jossey-Bass.

Videon, T. M., & Manning, C. K. (2003). Influences on adolescent eating patterns: The importance of family meals. *Journal of Adolescent Health, 32,* 365–373.

Visser, M. (1991). *The rituals of dinner: The origins, evolutions, eccentricities, and meanings of table manners.* New York: Penguin Books.

Weizman, Z. O., & Snow, C. E. (2001). Lexical input as related to children's vocabulary acquisition: Effects of sophisticated exposure and support for meaning. *Developmental Psychology, 37,* 265–279.

Zollo, P. (1999). *Wise up to teens: Insights into marketing and advertising to teenagers* (2nd ed.). Ithaca, NY: New Strategist Publications.

REED W. LARSON *holds the Pampered Chef Endowed Chair in Family Resiliency in the Department of Human and Community Development at the University of Illinois in Urbana-Champaign and is a professor in the Departments of Psychology and Educational Psychology.*

KATHRYN R. BRANSCOMB *is a doctoral student in the Department of Human and Community Development at the University of Illinois in Urbana-Champaign.*

ANGELA R. WILEY *is an assistant professor of applied family studies and an extension specialist at the University of Illinois in Urbana-Champaign.*

NEW DIRECTIONS FOR CHILD AND ADOLESCENT DEVELOPMENT • DOI 10.1002/cad

2

The ideal of the proper family mealtime, originally devised by the Victorian middle class, gained cultural hegemony in modern America, but with the partial exception of the 1950s, only a minority of American families could ever live by it.

"Everyone Would Be Around the Table": American Family Mealtimes in Historical Perspective, 1850–1960

Simone Cinotto

In her article "The Key to Family Cohesion: Finding Time to Eat Together," columnist Jane Eisner (2002) put the question straight:

> The repetitive nature of family meal times is the perfect conduit for the type of predictable but unstructured communication that leads to better parenting and healthier kids. One therapist in Connecticut even prescribes family dinners to the children she treats. But as a society, do we follow this advice? Of course not. An ongoing study . . . estimates that fewer than half of children ages 9 to 14 eat with their families every night. Other research shows a one-third drop in regular family meals during the last 25 years [p. A39].

Eisner's cry of alarm is in no way unusual. Many of the more pessimistic views on the contemporary American family refer to the decline of the family mealtime as both a proof and a cause of "family collapse." Such claims necessarily rely on historical presumptions, as they implicitly or explicitly project the image of a past when "things were not the way they are today." Denunciations such as Eisner's assume that before the current "crisis," there had been a more or less historically static, widely shared pattern of regular family meals. They also imply that the meanings and functions attached to eating rituals in the family have remained constant and

NEW DIRECTIONS FOR CHILD AND ADOLESCENT DEVELOPMENT, no. 111, Spring 2006 © Wiley Periodicals, Inc.
Published online in Wiley InterScience (www.interscience.wiley.com) • DOI: 10.1002/cad.152

recognizable over time and—since class, race, and ethnic differences are seldom mentioned—that they cut across social boundaries.

Is this representation historically correct? Let us start by saying that what is really at stake here is a model, an idealized image of what the domestic organization of meals should look like, and an image of the past as the place where that ideal was supposedly fulfilled. In order to check the claim that the traditional family mealtime is waning, we need to compare our current, historically constructed image of what constitutes a proper family meal with evidence from actual meals of the past.

Sociological literature on food provides ample evidence of current understandings of what ordered family meals are supposed to look like in the United States (Bell & Valentine, 1997). A proper family meal is one consumed in the home by family members. It is expected to be a daily routine. A proper family meal is homemade; unlike snacks or fast food, food is transformed in the domestic kitchen through a cultural operation (cooking), which requires time and effort. It entails planning on the part of the person in charge of cooking, and it is eaten at a regular time, according to an accepted set of rules and behaviors, including who sits where, what is discussed, and when one is allowed to leave the table. The mealtime has an important function in prioritizing family over other concerns: it requires working parents to set aside their work at a given time and children to set aside play or socializing. Family mealtimes are construed as important mechanisms of child rearing. Many Americans believe that family mealtimes actually "make" family, inasmuch as such social events "provide a basis for establishing and maintaining family culture, and . . . create a mutual recognition of the family as a group" (DeVault, 1991, p. 39). It is this vision of the everyday sharing of food within the domestic household that we need to examine and put in historical perspective here, because it is this ideal that makes up the memory of the traditional family mealtime "as it used to be."

The Cradle of the Proper Family Dinner: Family Mealtimes in Victorian Middle-Class Culture

The modern ideology and structure of family mealtimes found their origins in the culture of nineteenth-century Western European and American bourgeoisies. They are the result of economic changes conductive to separation of workplace and home, a more complex social stratification, and a novel differentiation and specialization of gender roles.

In colonial New England, the families of white independent farmers were at once a space of production, consumption, and social reproduction. The boundaries between the public and the private were also significantly permeable: the family actively participated in community life, and the community in turn exerted a significant control on family activities and behaviors. Within the family, the father ruled over his children with a patriarchal authority that embodied divine power and rested on his capacity to pass on to them land, property, and craft skills. Female submission was accordingly thought to be divinely prescribed and love between spouses a dispensable ingredient of marriage. Besides caring for the home and raising children, the wife of the independent farmer tended animals, worked in the fields, operated the loom, and performed other production tasks, just as her husband did (Mintz & Kellogg, 1988).

In such a family, food consumption was dictated by the sequence of daily activities, and hence, by natural, seasonal time. The mealtimes roughly consisted of a hearty "breakfast" taken early in the morning, before starting work; a midday "dinner," which was the most substantial repast of the day; and a lighter "supper," consumed after the work was done. However, this schedule was not formalized since the notion of the meal as a regular, structured activity of family life was at best vague. Early Americans of European descent felt free to eat wherever and whenever they could or wanted, in ways that resembled today's snacking (Gillis, 1996). Except for those of the wealthy, few American houses at the time of the Revolution had a designated space for meal consumption. In the standard house of Plymouth Colony, the "hall" was used for "cooking, eating, spinning, sewing, carpentry, prayer, schooling, entertaining, and even sleeping," occasionally at the same time (Demos, 1970, p. 39). The furniture of dining, consisting of a couple of boards set on trestles, was assembled for the meal and removed at the end of it. In many eighteenth-century American homes, a "family meal" bore little similarity to the later ideal. Although the entire family would eat in the same room at approximately the same time, only the men were permitted to take their meal seated. Women and children were likely to hastily swallow their food standing up, before resuming their previous undertakings (Gillis, 1996).

From the late eighteenth century, the patriarchal colonial family gradually began to shift toward the more self-reliant, democratic, and affectionate family pattern some historians characterize as the "modern family." This transition radically redefined the home dining habits of the upper and middle classes of businessmen and professionals.

Industrialization was an important cause of change, as it brought about the detachment of productive work from the home. Middle-class men became the sole producers of family wealth—independent economic actors competing with each other in the liberal, "godless" world of commerce, industry, and politics. Women's work became concealed in the home but achieved unprecedented social significance. Middle-class women were bestowed the burden of safeguarding a notion of domesticity that regarded the home as the realm of family privacy and intimacy. The ideology and the practice of the separate spheres thus turned the family into a special place where affectionate, noncontractual giving of services and gifts did occur. Children were now coming to be regarded as pliable individuals whose personalities could be molded by means of strategies more subtle than physical intimidation, such as through example, internalization through repetition, and the instillation of a sense of guilt. Infusing children with values of responsibility, order, and self-discipline, which would prepare them to compete and succeed in the larger society, became one of the primary purposes of middle-class family life (Mintz & Kellogg, 1988).

As the functions of the family became mostly psychological and ideological, family rituals became more important, dotting the yearly calendar and regulating the daily routine of family life. It was exactly then that the "traditional family meal" was created. In the Victorian middle-class family, meals became special occasions that occurred every day. They became social events that linked good manners and social status, organized people and activities in the family, and reinforced an elaborate ideology of group solidarity, concern for individuality, and clear gender differentiation.

The creation of an ordered setting of promptly served meals was greatly facilitated by the diffusion of the clock in the 1840s. By the 1850s and 1860s, as standardized schedules of school and work began to impress their rhythms on middle-class family life, there had emerged a carefully ordered progression of breakfast, lunch, and dinner, which "marked off the middle class from the big lunch eaters down the social scale" (Gillis, 1996, p. 90). Punctuality, now a value in itself, was taught and enforced through the controlled sequence of mealtimes.

An impressive quantity of publications, cookbooks, and handbooks aimed at supervising and reforming family practices, such as best-selling Catharine E. Beecher and Harriet Beecher Stowe's *The American Woman's Home, or Principles of Domestic Science* (1869), helped shaping the process. This prescriptive literature served as a blueprint for many middle-class families to follow.

For the nineteenth-century middle class, breakfast was the most spontaneous and informal meal, allowing an amount of freedom that, according to John A. Ruth's *Decorum: A Practical Treatise on Etiquette and Dress of the Best American Society* (1882), "would be unjustifiable at any other time": the father might read the morning paper or the mail, and children might be permitted to leave the table "without waiting for a general signal." At noon, the substantial dinner of the rural family was substituted by a lighter lunch. On weekdays, in the absence of men and school-age children, lunch was often taken by only women and younger children. It might occasionally turn into a lunch party attended by a circle of married women friends, just as family men might consume work "luncheons" with their peers in restaurants and clubs.

Much of the ceremonialism that the Victorian middle class attached to food consumption concentrated on dinner, which, to accommodate urban work and school schedules, gradually moved from midday to evening. In the late nineteenth century, the increasingly suburban middle-class families finally ate dinner at seven o'clock, when commuting men had returned home. The ritual significance of dinner derived from its status as the only time of the day when all the family gathered in the presence of the father: the less time the family spent together, the more important that little time became. The format of the meal followed an eminently British model, with meat and two side vegetables as the main course and a final dessert.

The Victorian middle-class family also proceeded to formalize the spatial contours of family mealtimes. By the 1850s, the dining room had emerged as a new domestic space and a sure indicator of a family's attainment of middle-class respectability. As a separate, functionally specialized space for the consumption of family meals, the dining room was an architectural reflection of the importance of mealtimes in an effort to turn the house into a sacred refuge. Occupying the central position in the house, separated from the kitchen, the dining room came to epitomize the family room par excellence, conveying a sense of cohesiveness and spiritual unity. Its furnishings were chosen with special care, as they were designed to set the stage for the most important family ritual and demonstrate the wealth and the taste of the family (Williams, 1985).

In the highly class-conscious world of the late-nineteenth-century upper and middle classes, great attention was paid to refined manners, which were considered unequivocal markers of a family's respectability and distinction. The double meaning of "taste" inherent in the realm of dining—taste in food selection and taste in social behavior, in particular where the control of one's bodily appetites was concerned—rendered table manners a particularly significant indicator of refinement. Table manners furthermore represented an early opportunity to pass the middle-class qualities of self-control, restraint, and deferment of pleasure on to the younger generation. In her advice book *Home* (1835), New England novelist Catharine Sedgwick argued that mealtime offered children in the family "three lessons a day" (Shapiro, 1986, p. 17).

Every family member was supposed to be at the table on time, appropriately dressed, and nicely groomed. Conversation, a crucial element of mealtimes, was expected to be conducted in urbane tones and to revolve around instructive topics. The learning of etiquette began with the use of tableware, which, in the course of the nineteenth century, grew to an unprecedented level of sophistication (on occasion, the Victorian middle-class family table displayed a remarkable array of forks, knives, cups, and saucers for every imaginable purpose). Children were usually admitted to the family table at age eight or nine, when they were deemed able to grasp the verbal and unspoken lessons adults would teach them (Kasson, 1990).

A crucial component of the family mealtime pattern created by the Victorian middle class was its supposed superiority and exportability. Victorian middle-class reformers believed that the industrial urban society they viewed as essentially disorderly could be significantly restructured if their archetype of family life—including their notions about what, when, where, how, and with whom to eat—gained wide acceptance among other classes and social groups (Shapiro, 1986). In the long run, their efforts were quite successful from the point of view of ideological penetration. By the early twentieth century, as the middle class expanded to include the increasingly numerous white-collar workers, their proper family mealtime pattern was hegemonic: it was widely considered the paradigm any family had to weigh itself against, especially by those social groups more in need of respectability and social acceptance. Still, material and social circumstances prevented many American families among poorer social strata from attaining this middle-class ideal.

Three Times a Day: Black and White Workers' Family Mealtimes in Industrializing America

The experience of slavery and migration inevitably affected the development of African American family life and dining habits. In the South, freedom confronted the black family with more differentiated gender roles: the responsibilities of cooking and the other domestic duties became more clearly defined as women's obligations. But the vast majority of freed women continued to work outside the home for long hours. The sharecropper woman, in particular, had little time to prepare meals. Typically her day began very early in the morning with the preparation of breakfast, which she served either in the cabin or the fields, where she joined the other family members who were already at work. She stopped work at midmorning to collect the wood needed to cook the midday meal, which often consisted of reheated breakfast leftovers. In the afternoon, her routine of multiple chores would be repeated until supper-once again, a quickly assembled repeat of previous meals. Even if freed slaves invested much of their first earnings in kitchen utensils and tableware, the dining equipment that was customary in the middle-class home remained absent from sharecroppers' cabins. Very little formality was attached to meal consumption. The only occasions for elaborate cooking and festive dining were family reunions and certain times of the agricultural cycle (Jones, 1985).

Like other migrants to the city in the 1910s and 1920s, African Americans in northern urban centers transformed themselves from food producers into consumers, encountering brand-new mass-produced items, which they gradually incorporated in their traditional diet. While overcrowded housing and decrepit kitchens hardly made the preparation of meals any easier or their consumption more ceremonious, urban work and school schedules led to the reorganization of mealtimes' timetable and content. Dinner, eaten late in the evening when all or most of the family was home, incorporated the southern breakfast pattern (fried pork, chicken, or other meats) with the southern noontime dinner pattern (vegetables) into a single one, coming to resemble the middle-class dinner format (Jerome, 1980). However, the only significant similarities between eating habits in these two disconnected worlds were this and the practice of saying grace before and after dinner. Racism in hiring left many black men unemployed and channeled black women into domestic jobs. This, in addition to the high rates of mortality among black males, caused the proportion of black families headed by unmarried or widowed women to soar. Women often juggled to balance wage work with domestic chores and child care, with scant possibility of success. The frequent cohabitation of relatives outside the nuclear family and unrelated boarders was yet another structural factor differentiating urban poor black households' mealtimes from those of the middle class (Jones, 1985).

Until the World War I years, many poorer urban white workers were also unable to adopt the middle-class model of family mealtimes. Despite differences in religion, ethnicity, skill, and occupation, some common factors did link the ways in which white working-class families ate at the turn of the twentieth century. First, as in black homes, there was no discrete space for meal consumption. They cooked, ate, and entertained guests in the kitchen, and they often worked and sometimes even slept there too. Economic conditions also dictated the circumstances of the preparation and presentation and meals. With the possible exception of Sunday dinner, working-class family mealtimes were not highly structured affairs.

Second, economic pressures induced many working-class families to take in boarders. The boarding system allowed women's work to be transformed into income without the women leaving the home, but family mealtimes had to be adjusted to make room for the paying guests (Strasser, 1982). Finally, many white working-class women did work outside the home. At the turn of the twentieth century, it was close to customary for working-class girls to work from when they left school until they married, and significant percentages of women worked for a wage even after marriage. In 1912, a U.S. Senate report on the conditions of working women and children concluded that in mill towns throughout America, "the so-called normal family—father with wife and children dependent upon him for support—is not found" (Kessler-Harris, 1982, p. 122).

As a result, turn-of-the-century middle-class observers would note with dismay that in the lower-class houses they visited, "proper family meals were unheard of, and food was simply left on a bare table for family members to grab when they could" (Shapiro, 1986, p. 130). Social reformers denounced the damage that lower-class "practices" did to the proper family mealtime pattern and set out plans to "improve" the ways working-class families had their meals.

These observers soon concluded that home economics could be the perfect medium to win the "dangerous classes" to the cause of proper domesticity. This new discipline was originally aimed at middle-class housewives left with no domestic help by the flight of wage-earning white women from domestic service into the expanding manufacturing and clerical sectors. It developed from the positivist belief that every department of human affairs could be rationalized with a scientific approach and from the Victorian notion that the private domain of the home and the family was the foundation on which a healthy liberal and democratic society could possibly be built. College-trained domestic scientists instructed the middle-class wife how to optimize time and resources using methodical home organization and wise consumption of the new mass-produced consumer goods.

The defense and support of the proper family mealtime in the face of the "servant shortage" was one of home economics' main concerns (Strasser, 1982). In their efforts to address working-class dining habits, reformers proceeded from the Puritan conviction that poverty was more a product of the weaknesses of the poor than social injustice and the Victorian belief that "the well-run home [w]as the most powerful guardian of civil peace" (Shapiro, 1986, p. 131). Armed with this ideological gear, pools of social workers, philanthropists, doctors, nutritionists, and teachers set out "to educate the wives and daughters of working men to be more intelligent home makers." Books, women's magazines, and cooking classes were directed at a wide-ranging public of native and immigrant working-class women and men. In the early decades of the twentieth century, workers' families were systematically exposed to lessons in what a family mealtime should look like, the middle-class way.

This cultural pattern would have not been able to establish itself as the universal model to be strived for if transformations in food production and distribution had not at the same time enhanced the consuming power of American working people (Levenstein, 1988). The gradually expanding access to a richer diet during the 1910s and 1920s worked hand in hand with the dispersal of middle-class principles to transform the tables of workers, at least tentatively and on selected occasions, into sites for symbolic, ritualized performances of "family values." The millions of immigrants who remade the American working class at the turn of the twentieth century in particular drew from their encounter with American abundance the material for family eating rituals that functioned as arenas in which the conflicting but interconnected processes of Americanization and ethnicization took place.

Eating Out of the Melting Pot: Mealtimes in New Immigrant Families

While countless social, cultural, and gastronomic differences existed among different nationalities and ethnic groups, most turn-of-the-century immigrants faced similar dilemmas regarding the content, context, and meaning of family mealtimes in the United States. The new immigrants, many of whom came from rural settings, had to adapt their diet, mealtime schedule, and meal formats to a new marketplace, urban life and industrial work rhythms, and in some cases the difficulties of life on the frontier (Gabaccia, 1998).

NEW DIRECTIONS FOR CHILD AND ADOLESCENT DEVELOPMENT • DOI 10.1002/cad

Most important, the relocation to America implied a critical redefinition of power relations, gender roles, and generational behaviors inside the family. It was within this framework that immigrants typically endowed family mealtimes as "rituals of cohesiveness" that were aimed at negotiating between conflicting public and private claims, construing "traditional" and "modern" ways, and constantly reinventing the identity of the group, typically under the ideological banners of "authenticity" and "tradition."

In many Jewish (Diner, 2001), Japanese (Masuoka, 1945), Italian (Cinotto, 2001), and other immigrant families, "food fights" intertwined with tensions between immigrant parents and their American-born children. The status of immigrant parents—in particular, the patriarchal authority of the father—was often deeply shaken by the social circumstances of American life. The father, the unquestioned head of the household in the rural economy of the old country, was now often a non-English-speaking, unskilled wage worker, ranking low in social position in a society highly conscious of race. At the same time, wage work for the American-born children of immigrants was the gateway to individualization, and exposure to and participation in other institutions in the public realm—the school, the peer group, and mass popular culture—reinforced their cultural independence.

On the food terrain, while immigrant parents tended to cling to familiar, time-blessed foods and preparations, their children typically saw immigrant food habits as markers of social inferiority. The children of immigrants were the principal recipients and carriers of new "American" ideas about food and nutrition. In the early 1940s, for instance, a second-generation Japanese immigrant in Hawaii, working as a domestic servant in a white middle-class home, expressed a typical attitude regarding her parents' food habits: "I don't like Japanese foods, I don't know why. I don't like rice and fish. Fish smells bad and rice takes too long to cook" (Masuoka, 1945, p. 765).

In immigrant households, therefore, family mealtimes were often sites of confrontation. In her novel *Bread Givers* (1925), Anzia Yezierska contrasts the strict patriarchal behavior of a Jewish immigrant father during family mealtimes with his loss of any real influence over the family in the new social world of Manhattan's Lower East Side. His daughters turn to their mother as the most respected and reliable figure in the family.

Most frequently, however, the immigrant family table turned into a site of negotiation for conflicting generational demands and a conduit for the production of ethnic identity. In the interwar years, as it became evident that coercive discipline was no longer effective in controlling their children, immigrants increasingly refrained from interfering with the new ways the American born had adopted. But while they gave "consent" to their children to behave the "American way" in public, they resorted to ritual and symbolic tools of socialization in private. Between the 1920s and the 1940s, family mealtimes—in particular the religious feasts of Sunday dinner, Jewish

Friday night, and the Sabbath meal—emerged as the most important means of articulating a separate private ethnic sphere. The American abundance of food—which for many previously destitute immigrants was the most tangible reward that migration had delivered—allowed rich convivial events that brought the entire family together. The immigrant home developed into a private haven of ethnic traditionalism in a public world of American modernity. As the Italian American scholar Richard Gambino described his growing up in Brooklyn, "The major meal of the week was the one at which time and circumstances permitted the most leisurely and largest gathering of *la famiglia.* It was the Sunday *pranzo,* which began in midafternoon . . . and lasted until early evening. It is a relaxed social gathering of the clan, featuring intimate conversations as much as well-prepared courses" (1974, p. 22). The content of mealtimes, while not imperatively all ethnic, triggered discussions of traditional food and conviviality. Nostalgic storytelling and reminiscences of "the other side" served to communicate and celebrate traditional family values in a touching and convincing way. As Gambino remembered: "In a very poignant way, meals were a 'communion' of the family, and food was 'sacred' because it was the tangible medium of that communion" (1974, p. 17).

Immigrant children may have accepted the generational bargain involving the separation of public and private realms because participation in ethnically ritualized family mealtimes did not interfere with their public world, because they realized the importance of the family for their own survival, or because of their enduring bonds of affection for their parents and other foreign-born relatives: interiorization of traditional family values tended to follow anyway.

The new ideal of domesticity based on a clear separation of the ethnic home and the outside world, the emphasis on family mealtimes as a crucial child-rearing and ideological elaboration terrain, and the highlighting of the role of women as self-sacrificing guardians of the hearth and competent providers of well-prepared courses all represented significant engagements with middle-class cultural values. In form, if not in content and context, the ethnic proper family mealtime came to resemble the middle-class proper family mealtime. As such, it paradoxically represented a significant sign of Americanization.

During the 1940s, the European American ethnics, who had just been able to join the "roast beef and apple pie" confederacy, sometimes used the argument of the superiority of their domesticity to differentiate themselves from the poorer nonwhite groups they were encountering in growing numbers in their inner-city neighborhoods (Cinotto, 2001). Assertions of whiteness during postwar urban crisis also helped in transforming turn-of-the-century European immigrants and their children into true followers of the "proper family mealtime" credo.

World's Highest Standard of Living: Family Mealtimes from the 1920s Through World War II

By the 1920s, a new pattern of middle-class family life had emerged, one that emphasized a greater camaraderie among household members. Marriage was expected to fulfill companionship and sexual demands from both sexes. The extension of life expectancy caused marriages to last longer, but those that did not respond to initial expectations were terminated in rising numbers. Birthrates fell sharply, while a revolution in manners signaled the emergence of a more educated, independent, self-assertive "new woman." Middle-class women entered wage work in significant numbers as an effect of their new aspirations and the new positions opened to them in the labor market (Kessler-Harris, 1982).

Eating out also became a popular middle-class practice in response to these and other changes. Once a male-only experience, performed within either working-class saloons or upper-class hotel lounges, eating out was transformed by prohibition, which crushed both of those institutions. By the 1920s, many restaurants catered to the growing class of male and female clerical workers, and eating out had developed into a leisure-time activity for the entire family (Levenstein, 1988).

Under such circumstances, the ideal of the proper family mealtime was caught between a renewed emphasis on its place as the main ritual of family cohesiveness and a growing concern about the difficulty real families were having in meeting the standard. When Robert and Helen Lynd visited Muncie, Indiana, for their famous study on mid-America in the 1920s, *Middletown*, they found that "meal-time as family reunion time was taken for granted a generation ago; under the decentralizing pull of a more highly diversified and organized leisure—in which basket-ball games, high school clubs, bridge clubs, civic clubs, and Men's League dinners each drain off their appropriate members from the family groups—there is arising a conscious effort to 'save meal-times, at least, for the family.'" In other words, the daily family mealtime, carried out "the way it used to be," was more a cause for concern, a symbol of past family life to defend from change, and a product of wishful thinking than a lived reality. During a meeting of the Mothers' Council, one woman confessed, "Even if we have only a little time at home together, we want to make the most of that little. In our time we always try to have Sunday breakfast and dinner together at least." One father echoed uncomfortably: "I ate only seven meals at home all last week and three of those were on Sunday. It's getting so a fellow has to make a date with his family to see them" (1929, p. 153).

Consumerism and new forms of commercial leisure undermined the actual implementation of the "proper family mealtime" in Muncie. The rising appeal and necessity of eating out advanced the public consumption of

New Directions for Child and Adolescent Development • DOI 10.1002/cad

food over the home to an unprecedented extent. The Lynds described the automobile as "making noticeable inroads upon the traditional prestige of the family's mealtimes at certain points; it has done much to render obsolete the leisurely Sunday noon dinner of a generation ago, and during half the year when 'getting out in the car' is pleasant, it often curtails the evening meal to an informal 'bite'"(1929, p. 153).

During the subsequent fifteen years of depression and wartime, the gap between the conventional model and the reality of family mealtimes remained wide. Public discourses accentuating the emphasis on family mealtimes as important glue for an institution put at risk by the blows of exceptional hardships added to a sense of inadequacy on the part of the many families that could not live by the benchmark.

With the entry of the United States into World War II, the ideal acquired not only social but also patriotic meanings. American women, as responsible for the country's cooking during wartime, were expected to save food while concocting family meals. The government instituted major rationing programs and advised housewives on how to do their part in the war effort, using surplus items wisely and avoiding others. At the same time, government-supported wartime agencies took pains to support family mealtimes as a means of enhancing the physical and emotional well-being of American families. The Committee on Food Habits, for example, was concerned with implementing emergency measures allowing proper family dining in case of evacuation of cities: "Unless care is taken to make the meal a family meal, the cafeteria situation may contribute to the breakdown of family ties. If father, mother, and children are to eat in a cafeteria, small tables, family tickets, adequate allowance for young children, should all be made. Otherwise, the children, assured of meals, may form gangs and break away from parental control which is no longer reinforced by the ritual of family meals" (Bentley, 2002, p. 182).

Wartime propaganda insisted on the image of the proper family mealtime as a reassuring icon of social stability in a time of anxiety and turmoil. While domestic food shortages, the absence of men who were in the service, and the unprecedented numbers of full-time wage-working women were rending the opportunity for a proper family mealtime utopia for most Americans, comforting images of bountiful meals shared by entire families gathered at the dining room table, with women as cooks and servers, were ubiquitous in government propaganda. Such images advanced a twofold goal: reassuring Americans that American abundance was not at its twilight and restoring their confidence in the steadiness of the family, gender roles, and American society as a whole.

No other image served these ideas more effectively than Norman Rockwell's *Freedom from Want* painting. Originally appearing in the *Saturday Evening Post* in early 1943 as part of a series of paintings illustrating the "four freedoms" that President Roosevelt had invoked in his 1941 State of the Union Address, and reproduced and distributed by the millions by the Office of War Information, *Freedom from Want* depicts the quintessential American feast, Thanksgiving dinner. In the painting, a grandmotherly woman is serving a gargantuan, succulent turkey to a family group gathered at the table. On the two sides of the nicely set table, replete with all the trimmings, everybody is smiling. *Freedom from Want* was probably the most powerful illustration of the values conveyed by the traditional family mealtime to date, portrayed with strong patriotic overtones. To Americans hesitantly asking, "What are we fighting for?" Rockwell's image decisively responded: for country, the traditional family, material abundance, and our longstanding traditions and customs (Bentley, 2002).

Family Mealtimes on the Crabgrass Frontier: American Dinner in the 1950s

In the 1950s, more Americans than ever before or ever since achieved the dream meal that Norman Rockwell had so convincingly depicted. Thanks to a postwar economic boom, the middle class, as defined by a family income between three thousand and ten thousand dollars a year, doubled in size from 1929 to include three-fifths of Americans by the mid-1950s. Even some sectors of the working class enjoyed relative security and affluence for the first time in history. The postwar baby boom added 50 million children to the nation's population by the end of the 1950s. Divorce rates stabilized. The role of women in the family was further gendered. Women's magazines, psychologists, and a variety of other opinion makers asserted that child rearing and house management were their primary, full-time responsibilities. As expected by many American men, most women who had been working for a wage during the war relinquished their jobs, while most of their younger counterparts entered housewifery immediately after high school or college. The rush to the suburbs physically separated the male world of work from the female world of the home. The ideology of the separate spheres was never closer to its realization for greater numbers of people than it was in the 1950s. In 1950, 60 percent of American households conformed to the "male breadwinner/female full-time homemaker" form the Victorians had set as appropriate a century earlier (Mintz & Kellogg, 1988).

In a sizable number of American households, if not the majority, family mealtimes responded to the culturally hegemonic standard. A 1950 sociological study of rituals among urban and suburban white families found a broad observance of the model of a homemade dinner, cooked and served by the mother to the members of the nuclear family, featuring familial conversation and adherence to standard rules of behavior (Bossard & Boll, 1950). In general, there was still a lot of family diversity in the 1950s—most African American families did not participate in the affluence that was a factor in the "family of the fifties" phenomenon, for example—and class differences were only slightly less sharp than in the past, but social changes made differentiation at the family table proportionally less relevant than it had previously been.

Bossard and Boll (1950) noted that the value of breakfast and lunch as family rituals had significantly declined from the prewar period. The weekday breakfast, in particular, was apparently dying out as a structured meal. The sample families ate it as quickly as possible, either individually or as a group, and with little formality. Conversely, the researchers found that "dinner has been accented as a festive reunion meal," if in a context of persisting class differentiation. "In the lower-class family, the mother . . . does prepare the food, but the rest of the family comes and takes it when and where they want to. Some of these families never have a meal sitting down with the whole family together except for Sunday dinner, which is considered a very special occasion." The researchers argued that the reason for this "choice" was that in large families, there was not enough room to accommodate every person at the same time. In smaller households, the family did eat together, although the use of the dining room—for families that could afford one—might have been reserved for Sunday dinner and holidays, the family preferring to eat in the kitchen during the week. Middle-class dinner in many cases "involve[d] very formal procedures. It [was] at a certain time, usually six or six-thirty" (Bossard & Boll, 1950, p. 116). The presence of the whole family at the table was prescribed, and dinner took place predominantly in the dining room. Each member of the family had a special place to sit, and the assignment of different roles to different family members was often formalized. The mother served, the father carved, the son cleared the table, and the daughter did the dishes. Significant attention was also paid to the setting of the table and the uses of dinnerware, in sharp contrast with the much more informal meals of the day.

In many households, dinnertime, dictated by the time of the father's return from work, was the only occasion during which the whole family would be together and thus its most crucial daily ritual. Such centrality had significant implications for the role expectations of women in American society. The preparation of the evening meal was, aside from caring for children, the most important and identity-defining daily activity of many women. As cooks and housewives in the 1950s, women were expected to be "modern," wise consumers of the proliferating mass-produced convenience foods and kitchen appliances, while still serving as "traditional" care providers. At the same time, more than ever before, women were made to feel guilty if they worked for a wage to meet rising family needs, as they increasingly did toward the end of the 1950s. The uneasy balance between the self-realization of the woman as bread giver and the frustrations inherent in an exclusive commitment to domestic undertakings was one of the unspoken tensions underlying the rosy appearance of the suburban middle-class family dinner of the 1950s (Shapiro, 2004).

In the history of American society, the family of the 1950s was an exception brought about by a convergence of factors—early marriage, large families, and stable divorce rates in the context of a booming industrial consumer economy—that had never happened before and is not likely ever to happen again. And even then there was much diversity in the way Americans organized their family life and mealtimes. One of the reasons that that brief historical period is popularly renowned for epitomizing traditional domesticity and traditional family mealtimes is that the media have widely depicted it that way. Popular television series such as *Father Knows Best, Leave It to Beaver,* and *Ozzie and Harriet* offered numerous representations of family dinners during which characters shared discussion of everyday problems, got lessons in life from a breadwinning dad, and were served a homemade delicious meal from a mom in pearls and shirtwaist dresses. The first generation of television viewers grew up being massively exposed to images of family mealtimes as celebration of the traditional domestic division of labor and family ideology; their children, who had no firsthand memory of the period, appreciated it nostalgically even so through retro representations such as *Happy Days* and countless others (Leibman, 1995). Confounding idealized visions of family life conveyed by media representations with the actual past may be a source of painful contrasts between expectations and lived reality.

Conclusion: The Legacy of Modern Family Mealtimes to Postmodern Families

By the late 1950s, the economic, social, and cultural changes that would dramatically alter the characteristic family pattern of the postwar era in the decades to come were already set in motion. The emergent postindustrial economy drew more nonunionized and cheaper female labor into the expanding clerical and service sectors. Rising consumption standards, mass collegiate education, and escalating divorce rates attracted growing numbers of working- and middle-class mothers into paid labor, thoroughly changing the social framework in which the model of parenthood of the 1950s had developed. From a cultural point of view, the tensions underlying the happy facade of the family of the 1950s emerged powerfully in the 1960s and 1970s, radically transforming women's and young people's conception of gender roles. That transformation complicated the way Americans looked to the family for their emotional fulfillment and personal welfare (Mintz & Kellogg, 1988).

As differences in family life have prevailed again after the brief and partial interval of the 1950s, mealtimes have had to adapt to changing economic, social, and cultural conditions. Other chapters in this volume conclude that the homemade meal prepared by a full-time female homemaker is much less common now than it was fifty years ago. The food might be "cooked by the phone," that is, home delivered, the television is on, and the family may include only one adult. Still, authors have found wide, transcultural consensus among Americans today on the value of mealtimes as a means of family cohesion and children acculturation, and many families do share an evening meal together at least some nights of the week. Some of them make great efforts to do so.

The idealized image of the traditional family mealtime seems to have endured the transition to a late- or postmodern society admirably well. The historical analysis delineated in this chapter suggests that the great resiliency of this ideal lies in its capacity to convey the idea of stability in times of crisis and change. The proper family mealtime pattern has typically been at hand for various social groups (or social actors inside them) in need of redefining the relations of power within the family and the role of the family within society at a particular historical moment.

Of course, different families have always had their particular understanding of what "proper" meant, class, race, and ethnicity all being influential factors. And even more significant an issue in the practice of and public debates on family mealtimes is gender. From its Victorian inception, the gendered organization of the proper family mealtime has always centered around the control of women's unpaid labor in the home as a cook and server. A middle-class ideal, the notion of the bread-giving wife as guardian of the home, was promptly embraced by men in the nascent industrial working class, less prone to bourgeois cultural influence than interested in maintaining the prerogatives they had always enjoyed. Since then, unionized male workers have struggled for wage gains that would allow them to keep their wives home, caring for children and preparing dinner, as an integral part of the American dream. Middle-class reformers and opinion shapers, for their part, denounced wage-working women as a threat to the stability of the family, on the basis that they were unable to provide their traditional support to the institution, obviously including with that the preparation and serving of meals. From the mid-nineteenth to the mid-twentieth century, all public discourse on the proper family mealtime inevitably relied on the expectation, hope, or obligation that women would be home to cook it.

As can be seen, the modern ideal of the proper family mealtime has had a peculiar history. An example of Eric Hobsbawm's famous theorization of the "invention of tradition" (1983), the traditional American family mealtime is a recent creation, being less than two hundred years old. It was a minority group—the Victorian middle class—that invented the family mealtime mystique in America. Yet the actual implementation of that original ideal has historically been more the exception than the rule. Most American families, with the partial exception of the 1950s, have been largely unsuccessful in trying to meet it. Such a gap has recurrently raised lively public debate, and many influential observers have vocally expressed concern about its social costs. In fact, the perception of the proper family mealtime as a traditional practice jeopardized by social change so popular in the media today has been itself part of the picture for a very long time. Nevertheless, the core ideal formalized by the nineteenth-century urban and suburban middle class has shown remarkable resilience and flexibility over time, constituting a crucial feature of diverse ideologies of the family, especially during periods of social and cultural change. Although the actual practice of family mealtimes has continually strived to meet different cultural and economic circumstances, the idealized image of the proper family mealtime—family members gathered around the table, enjoying familial food and intimate conversation—has been a remarkably constant symbol of unity and stability for the American family.

References

Beecher, C. E., & Beecher Stowe, H. (1869). *The American woman's home, or principles of domestic science.* New York: J. B. Ford & Co.

Bell, D., & Valentine, G. (1997). *Consuming geographies: We are what we eat.* New York: Routledge.

Bentley, A. (2002). Islands of serenity: The icon of the ordered meal in World War II. In C. Counihan (Ed.), *Food in the U.S.A.: A reader* (pp. 171–192). New York: Routledge.

Bossard, J., & Boll, E. J. (1950). *Ritual in family living: A contemporary study.* Philadelphia: University of Pennsylvania Press.

Cinotto, S. (2001). "Sunday dinner? You had to be there!" The social significance of food in Italian Harlem, 1920–1940. *Italian American Review, 8,* 11–44.

Demos, J. (1970). *A little commonwealth: Family life in Plymouth Colony.* New York: Oxford University Press.

DeVault, M. L. (1991). *Feeding the family: The social organization of caring as a gendered work.* Chicago: University of Chicago Press.

Diner, H. R. (2001). *Hungering for America: Italian, Irish, and Jewish foodways in the age of migration.* Cambridge, MA: Harvard University Press.

Eisner, J. (2002, December 26). The key to family cohesion: Finding time to eat together. *Philadelphia Inquirer,* p. A39.

Gabaccia, D. R. (1998). *We are what we eat: Ethnic food and the making of Americans.* Cambridge, MA: Harvard University Press.

Gambino, R. (1974). *Blood of my blood: The dilemma of the Italian-Americans.* New York: Anchor Press.

Gillis, J. R. (1996). *A world of their own making: Myth, rituals, and the quest for family values.* New York: Basic Books.

Hobsbawm, E. (1983). Introduction: Inventing traditions. In E. Hobsbawm & T. Ranger (Eds.), *The invention of tradition* (pp. 1–14). Cambridge: Cambridge University Press.

Jerome, N. W. (1980). Diet and acculturation: The case of black-American in-migrants. In N. W. Jerome, R. F. Kandel, & G. H. Pelto (Eds.), *Nutritional anthropology: Contemporary approaches to diet and culture* (pp. 275–325). Pleasantville, NY: Redgrave Publishing Co.

Jones, J. (1985). *Labor of love, labor of sorrow: Black women, work, and the family from slavery to the present.* New York: Vintage Books.

Kasson, J. (1990). *Rudeness and civility: Manners in nineteenth century America.* New York: Hill and Wang.

Kessler-Harris, A. (1982). *Out to work: A history of wage-earning women in the United States.* New York: Oxford University Press.

Leibman, N. C. (1995). *Living room lectures: The fifties family in film and television.* Austin: Texas University Press.

Levenstein, H. A. (1988). *Revolution at the table: The transformation of the American diet.* New York: Oxford University Press.

Lynd, R. S., & Lynd, H. M. (1929). *Middletown: A Study in modern American culture.* Orlando, FL: Harcourt.

Masuoka, J. (1945). Changing food habits: The Japanese in Hawaii. *American Sociology Review, 10,* 759–765.

Mintz, S., & Kellogg, S. (1988). *Domestic revolutions: A social history of American family life.* New York: Free Press.

Ruth, J. A. (1883). *Decorum: A practical treatise on etiquette and dress of the best American society.* New York: Union Publishing House.

Shapiro, L. (1986). *Perfection salad: Women and cooking at the turn of the century.* New York: Modern Library.

Shapiro, L. (2004). *Something from the oven: Reinventing dinner in 1950s America.* New York: Viking.

Strasser, S. (1992). *Never done: A history of American housework.* New York: Holt.

Williams, S. (1985). *Savory suppers and fashionable feasts: Dining in Victorian America.* New York: Pantheon Books.

Yezierska, A. (1925). *Bread givers.* New York: Arno Press.

SIMONE CINOTTO *is a member of the Piero Bairati Center for Euro-American Studies, University of Turin.*

3

Two anthropologists treat mealtimes as cultural sites for socializing children into commensality, communicative expectations, and the symbolic, moral, and sentimental meanings of food and eating. Using ethnographic evidence, they indicate how mealtime comportment is embedded in practices and ideologies relevant to children's competent membership in their families and communities.

The Cultural Structuring of Mealtime Socialization

Elinor Ochs, Merav Shohet

Anthropologists have long considered ways in which food preparation, distribution, and consumption authenticate both social order and moral and aesthetic beliefs and values. Less frequently examined are the socialization processes that promote continuity and change across generations in the sociocultural life of food.

This chapter considers mealtimes as cultural sites for the socialization of persons into competent and appropriate members of a society. Cultural sites are here conceptualized as historically durable yet transformable, socially organized and organizing, and tempospatially situated arenas, which are laden with symbolic meanings and mediated by material artifacts. Cultural sites are given life through recurrent social participation and longevity through efforts to socialize novices into the predilections, sentiments, and actions that undergird meaningful participation. This notion of cultural site assumes that members will act in conventional ways, yet not necessarily share common understandings and knowledge of the situation at hand (Eagleton, 2000; Garfinkel, 1967; Geertz, 1973; Sapir, 1993). It follows Bourdieu in approaching culture as an ever changing set of dispositions, strategies, and social positions that members contingently enact in relation to one another within situations and fields of local relevance (1977, 1990a, 1990b).

With this notion of cultural site in mind, mealtimes can be regarded as pregnant arenas for the production of sociality, morality, and local understandings of the world. Mealtimes are both vehicles for and end points of

culture. As vehicles, mealtimes constitute universal occasions for members not only to engage in the activities of feeding and eating but also to forge relationships that reinforce or modify the social order. In addition, mealtimes facilitate the social construction of knowledge and moral perspectives through communicative practices that characterize these occasions. Yet mealtimes are also objects of cultural import in themselves. They are more or less conventional and demarcated as a kind of social practice that requires certain sensibilities of participants. Mealtimes vary within and across social groups in relation to participation, setting, duration, meal items, meal sequence, and attributed significance.

These considerations inform the cultural structuring of mealtime socialization. Rather than a bundle of mealtime traits, customs, symbols, and rules that experts transmit and children and other novices come to master, cultural knowledge and practices associated with mealtimes are recreated and altered through socially and experientially asymmetrical relationships. A good deal of scholarship has been devoted to eliminating an either-or approach to culture and nature. These approaches instead emphasize mutually organizing influences, wherein culture pervades the development of children, while children are endowed with the agentive capacity to appropriate culture within their own frames for thinking, feeling, and acting in the world (Cole & Cole, 1996; LeVine, 1999; Mead, 1934; Rogoff, 1990).

Two processes are central to the cultural structuring of mealtime socialization: apprenticeship and language socialization. Apprenticeship is learning through active observation and direct participation in activities together with a more knowledgeable participant (Lave & Wenger, 1991; Rogoff, 1990). Apprenticeship is embedded in and organized by community ideologies and social arrangements for learning. This chapter considers ways in which families and communities may apprentice children into mealtime practices by soliciting their attention and involvement and positioning them as either observers and overhearers or as more central participants (for example, as mealtime preparers, servers, consumers, or communicators).

Language socialization is the process by which children and other novices acquire sociocultural competence through language and other semiotic modalities (Garrett & Baquedano-Lopez, 2002; Kulick & Schieffelin, 2004; Ochs & Schieffelin, 1984, 1995). Through mealtime communication, more experienced participants engage less experienced interlocutors in the collaborative construction of social order and cultural understandings. In some cases, the sociocultural messages are conveyed explicitly to the less experienced participants through speech activities such as directives, error corrections, and assessments. In other cases, sociocultural orientations are socialized through less direct strategies such as irony, inference, pragmatic presupposition, metaphor, and noticeable silences. Both direct and indirect communicative strategies can co-occur in the same mealtime and can be embedded in genres such as prayer, storytelling, and planning at the meal.

Socialization into Commensality

Commensality is the practice of sharing food and eating together in a social group such as a family. Universally, commensality is central to defining and sustaining the family as a social unit. In ancient Greece, for example, *oikos* (family) was stipulated as "those who feed together" (Lacey, 1968, p. 15). Similarly, on the Micronesian island of Fais, the family roles of father and mother are rooted in the mealtime functions of provider and preparer of food, and extended family relationships are maintained through redistribution of important food items such as yams (Rubinstein, 1979). Fais children are socialized into the importance of food sharing in the family unit through accompanying others in continuous cross-household visits that involve preparing, offering, and consuming food. Children are also warned to eat only with close relatives or face dire consequences.

While commensality is considered essential to sociality in many social groups, everyday realities indicate that members are not always eager to share their food items. Among the Kaluli of Papua New Guinea, for example, young children are socialized through prompting to obtain food from another person either by issuing a demand or by appealing to the person to feel sorry for them (Schieffelin, 1990). Similarly, one of the first words that young Samoan children produce is the affect-marked first-person pronoun *ita* (poor me), which they use to beg for food. Samoan children acquire this word before the neutral form of the first-person pronoun (Ochs, 1988), indicating the pragmatic role of food sharing in language development. On Fais island, children who fail to notice when food is ready may be taunted and find nothing left to eat (Rubinstein, 1979). They become wary of how food is distributed and display "a pattern of covert grumbling and gossip over others' stinginess or greed" (p. 211). In Northern Vietnam, as in other patriarchal societies, gender plays a role in food distribution: girls are reprimanded for their greed, while boys come to expect prime selections of food (Rydstrom, 2003).

In many communities, commensality involves eating together at the same time. For at least the past three decades, the ideal in the United States and Western Europe has been for family members to come together for the evening meal (Dreyer & Dreyer, 1973; Murcott, 1982; Ochs, Pontecorvo, & Fasulo, 1996). When children violate this ideal by beginning to eat before all family members are seated at the table, they may be explicitly reprimanded, as in the American family dinner interaction below (Ochs & Capps, 2001, p. 233):

MOTHER: (*agitated*) Come on. Don't start eating yet. You know better . . . (*All kids keep eating*) Put your forks down. Come on. Can't you have some manners? (*Mom checks to see if Jimmy and then Laurie are seated properly, pushing their chairs in.*) Put your forks down.

NEW DIRECTIONS FOR CHILD AND ADOLESCENT DEVELOPMENT • DOI 10.1002/cad

LAURIE: I wanna pray. (*clasps her hands*) Jesus? . . . Jesus?
MOTHER: Wait a minute Laurie. (*irritated, throwing arms up in semi-despair*) I'm not sitting down.

Dinnertime where everyone sits at a common table is a vanishing ideal for many families in the United States, in the face of busy schedules of working parents and highly engaged children involved in a plethora of extracurricular activities that leave little room for commensality. In their study of American family dinnertimes during the 1980s, Ochs, Smith, and Taylor (1989) found that mothers and children sometimes dined before the father returned home, or that children ate before their parents, often while watching television. Even when families managed to eat together, children often wanted to leave the dinner table as soon as possible rather than linger and interact with their parents, leading to extended negotiations about obligations to remain together at the meal.

In other communities, the ideal is not for family members to always eat together. Rather, children are socialized into commensality that involves a social order whereby certain members eat before others, according to generation, gender, or social rank. In China, for example, older-generation family members take food before the younger generation, and "on formal occasions when guests are present, children may even be excluded from the dining table until the adults are finished, or seated at a table separate from the adults" (Cooper, 1986, p. 181). In Samoa, older children are expected to help young untitled adults to prepare and serve meals. During important meals, older, titled adults generally eat the main meal before untitled adults and children, although they may bring a very young child next to them to share their food (Ochs, 1988). During more intimate family mealtimes, adults and children may eat at the same time. A similar pattern holds for the egalitarian Matsingenka, who dwell in the Peruvian Amazon, where men eat before women and children when several family units assemble, but in smaller nuclear family meals, the entire family eats at the same time (Izquierdo, 2001).

Families and communities also differ in moral and social priorities surrounding quality and amount of food according to generation, gender, and social rank. For example, in a study of Italian family mealtimes, parents favored children over themselves in the distribution of food (Ochs et al., 1996; Sterponi, 2002). In contrast, in the United States, parents emphasize that children should not take food at the expense of other family members but rather should leave enough for all, as illustrated below:

MOTHER: (*quite annoyed*) Adam? There are other people at this table. Now you put back two of those peaches! (*0.6 second pause*)
ADAM: Okay okay.

As indicated above, socialization into commensality is also socialization into sociocultural embodiments of generation, gender, and other social positionings. Embedded in the socialization of commensality are messages regarding the morality of food distribution and consumption and the rights of adults and children to determine how, when, and how much family members will eat.

Socialization into Food as Symbol and Tool

In every society, food is highly symbolic, in the sense that members imbue particular kinds and qualities of food with sentimental, moral, religious, and health-related meanings. Adults and children can also use food as a symbol of communal identity over historical time as well as to affirm or diminish affection and social bonds. A number of studies have reviewed the symbolic significance of food and eating among different social groups (Bourdieu, 1984; Douglas, 1975; Farb & Armelagos, 1980; Goody, 1982; Mintz & Du Bois 2002); less attention has been devoted to the practices through which children come to regard food as charged with specific sociocultural meanings.

Children's development is often linked to contact with or avoidance of particular foods. While breast milk universally is a possible, if not desirable, food item offered to infants, all children are eventually weaned. In the highlands of Indonesia, for example, this is accomplished by mothers enforcing a separation from the nursing child. Later in life, children assert their autonomy while reclaiming the privileges of early childhood by "stealing" foods from village fields (Hollan & Wellenkamp, 1996). In Papua New Guinea, Kaluli mothers keep children away from taboo foods that are thought to interfere with their mobility and social and language development. Rather than directly refusing a child's request for prohibited food, Kaluli mothers distract or fool children or prompt them to tell others, "I don't eat x," thereby encouraging them to take responsibility for the food taboo (Schieffelin, 1990, p. 69).

At mealtimes, different aspects of the food may be accentuated in different social groups. A comparative study of U.S. and Italian dinnertime socialization, for example, found that U.S. parents urged children to eat their meal, emphasizing that it is nutritious and part of a social contract, which yields a reward, namely, dessert. Italian parents emphasized food as a pleasure over the above three attributes in conversing with children about the meal (Ochs et al., 1996). The U.S. parental emphasis on food as nutrition and eating as a social and moral obligation led to protracted food negotiations and tensions at the dinner table, as illustrated below (pp. 14–16):

FATHER: If you don't eat a good dinner you won't . . . get any either. But I'm especially concerned about eating your vegetables, okay? They have minerals in them.

NEW DIRECTIONS FOR CHILD AND ADOLESCENT DEVELOPMENT • DOI 10.1002/cad

. . .

JANIE: I would like to leave this (*pointing to one item on plate*).
FATHER: Eat the vegetables? (*looking down at Janie's plate*)

. . .

JANIE: And eat that (*pointing to another item on plate, looking up at Father*) and eat three vitamins.

. . .

FATHER: You eat one piece of corn and two pieces of the green . . . some broccoli (*pause*) and you eat all that (*points to plate*) and take three vitamins.

In cases as the above, children's compliance with eating their meal dominated mealtime interaction. Such a here-and-now topical focus may preclude children from participating in mealtime discussions that would expose them to family and community frameworks for interpreting past and future events.

Socializing children into food as a reward focused in the United States exclusively on the dessert. As in the warning below (Ochs et al., 1996, p. 22), parents use dessert as a carrot or a stick to get children to eat the main portion of the meal, framing meat and vegetables as food the children must eat while dessert is cast as food the children want to eat:

FATHER: Whoever does not finish their vegetables does not get any ice cream for dessert.

The emphasis on dessert as a reward competes with the purported value of food as nutrition. In other words, some U.S. parents articulate mixed messages about the goodness of food. A separate study of U.S. middle-class families evidenced this contradiction at the family dinner table, as illustrated below (Izquierdo & Paugh, 2003, p. 9):

SANDRA: (*asking for lemonade*) Mommy please?
FATHER: Drink your milk first. You heard Mom.

. . .

LAURA: Mommy? (*pause*) Can I have Coke mixed (*pause*) with milk?
FATHER: Yeah (*pause*) yeah.

In contrast, Italian family dinners in the study did not include a dessert, and Italian parents did not use sweets to cajole children to eat. Indeed, Italian parents did not expect children to eat everything on the table; rather, they assumed that children, like adults, develop tastes and preferences for certain food items as part of their personalities and sought to affirm these preferences. Adults and children alike in the Italian dinners used a rich grammar of positive affect to praise both the food and the person who prepared or purchased it. In the excerpt below, for example, a child augments the word *pezzo* (piece) with the diminutive, affect-loaded suffixes *etto* (nice little) and *ino* (little) to form the word *pezzettino* in requesting a piece of meat (Ochs et al., 1996, p. 28):

CHILD: Mamma questo pezzettino lo voglio
[Mamma this appealing nice, little, delicate piece, I want it].

In addition to commending the food and its preparer or purchaser, parents at the Italian family dinners would also recount their own positive childhood memories of particular dishes on the dinner table. In this manner, food items were not only imbued with positive sentiments but also served to link family members across generations, and in some cases to bring family members no longer alive into family members' consciousness.

Invoking spirits of ancestors in the consumption of food is common across many societies, where children and other family members are enjoined to partake of food as a means of reinforcing the continuity of the family (Bloch, 1985; Feeley-Harnik, 1994; Watson, 1987). The emphasis on continuity of traditional foods contrasts with the practices of many families in the United States, where new foods are constantly introduced to children during mealtimes. Such novelty introduces stress at meals, both when parents express uncertainty over whether their children will eat the food they have prepared or purchased ("I don't know if the kids'll really like it") and when children indeed refuse to try something new (Ochs et al., 1996, p. 36).

Regardless of whether food is explicitly used to link present and past generations, it operates as a symbol of care in all social groups, yet at the same time it can be used as a weapon or threat. Mealtimes can thus be cultural sites for socializing children into conflict, for example, when children refuse others' attempts to get them to eat, when others reject children's demands for a desired food, or when alignments between family members are formed around food preferences and dispreferences.

Eating disorders such as anorexia and compulsive overeating are associated with issues of care and control in the family. In the case of anorexia, rejection of food is literally and figuratively a rejection of others' care and control (Katzman & Lee, 1997). Though anorexia is multi-determined, its increasing prevalence (Anderson-Fye & Becker, 2003) may be socialized in childhood and throughout the life span through gender- and class-related mass media messages about body norms and eating practices (Bordo, 1993). A sociocultural perspective may shed light on eating disorders, in that these messages are embedded in local ideologies about food and the body. These messages have been exported to and appropriated by social groups in which anorexia was not formerly manifest (Anderson-Fye & Becker, 2003). Often treatment of eating disorders involves clinical attempts to resocialize sufferers through a variety of modalities into different sensibilities about food and the body that are less self-destructive. Those undergoing resocialization, however, may find these attempts infuriating and infantilizing and reject intervention (Gremillion, 2003; Shohet, 2004).

Socialization into Mealtime Communication

Mealtimes are cultural sites not only for eating but also for communication. Who participates in which kinds of communicative practices during mealtimes is linked to historically rooted ideologies and practices. In addressing children's socialization into mealtime communication, it is important to consider both norms of appropriate mealtime communication and the social positioning of children in mealtime communication.

Norms of communication may include the norm that all participants will largely remain silent during the course of the meal, as among the Matsigenka of the Peruvian Amazon (Izquierdo, 2001). Alternatively, in some families and communities, children are expected to generally remain silent while adults converse, as in the adage, "Children are to be seen and not heard." A study of New England family mealtimes found that parents significantly dominated the conversation, with children producing only one-third of the talk (Dreyer & Dreyer, 1973). A study of urban Swedish family mealtimes similarly found that parents dominated conversation, with mothers providing more than half of all comments at the dinner table (De Geer, 2004). In societies where children are expected to be silent or eat separately or are positioned as servers, minimal or no communication may be directed to them, but they may nonetheless acquire critical sociocultural knowledge and skills through observing and overhearing the communication of others.

If there is communicative activity at mealtimes, children are socialized through different communicative roles into norms for participating in different kinds of mealtime genres considered appropriate by family and community. Children may assume different forms of participation such as author (person who composes message), animator (person who utters message), principal (person whose views are represented), recipient (person to whom message is directed), and overhearer (nonrecipient who attends to communicative activity) (Goffman, 1981). Across social groups, expectations concerning children's communicative roles take into account a child's developmental competence as well as the semiotic activity at hand.

In examining children's socialization into mealtime communication, we focus on children's participation in the construction of moral discourse. It is striking how not only feasts and rituals but also everyday family meals are rich cultural sites for reaffirming moral sentiments of the family and community. Mealtimes are pervaded by talk oriented toward reinforcing what is right and wrong about both the family and outsiders. Morality is socialized through grammatical markings of deference and authority, directives, assessments, justifications, excuses, apologies, prayers, storytelling, and other forms of communicative exchange in which children participate.

Children's table manners, for example, have been a focus of moral socialization across historical times and social groups. Elias's classic *The Civilizing Process* (2000), for example, documents how sixteenth-century texts were devoted to instructions concerning how French, German, and Italian elite children were to use their napkins and utensils, receive offers of food, and cut and chew meat. In contemporary times as well, families imbue children's mealtime comportment with moral meanings. We have illustrated U.S. children's socialization through and into the moral discourse of comportment in excerpts presented earlier in this chapter. North Vietnamese village families as well chastise young children, especially girls, for lapses in their comportment, for example, for failing to use chopsticks correctly, sit still and attentively, eat fast with concentration, or otherwise fail to display respect (Rydstrom, 2003). Similarly, Chinese children are socialized to display deference through eating every grain of rice in their bowl and not displaying a strong preference for certain favorite dishes by taking more than others (Cooper, 1986; Hsu & Hsu, 1977).

An important component of children's mealtime comportment may involve displaying appropriate engagement in mealtime prayers. In the United States, for example, children in certain families are expected to lead, join in, or say their own grace at the start of the meal. Dreyer and Dreyer (1973) observed that usually the oldest child led grace in families in which this genre was part of the mealtime practice. Children may be sanctioned when saying grace inappropriately, as illustrated earlier when Laurie began saying grace before her mother was seated. Similarly, in the example below, young David, in the middle of singing a Johnny Appleseed grace (from an enthusiastic children's song that gives thanks for "the sun, the rain and the apple seed"), suddenly opens his eyes, throws a fork on the floor, and switches to the Beatles' song "Maxwell's Silver Hammer" (Capps & Ochs, 2002, p. 46):

DAVID: BANG! BANG! Maxwell's silver fork!

His father models appropriate conduct by continuing to sing the Johnny Appleseed grace, while his mother quietly reprimands him:

FATHER: (*singing*) Thank the Lord.
MOTHER: (*softly*) Throwing hands aren't praying hands.

When David then laughingly shouts, "TIME FOR MAXWELL," his mother presses his hands together in prayer position and rejoins singing grace. These verbal and nonverbal maneuvers appear to have a positive outcome, as David also joins his parents in finishing the grace with a series of loud "AMEN! AMEN, AMEN, AMEN!"

For many social groups, family mealtimes are cultural sites for recounting narratives that convey moral messages. That is, exchanging accounts of personal or collective significance is often a central facet of the meal, as important as the food consumed. While in some cases, one family member dominates as narrator, in other cases, the narratives and the moral points they highlight are collaboratively produced by family members, including children (Ochs & Taylor, 1992). In a study comparing Jewish American and Israeli family mealtime narratives, Blum-Kulka (1997, p. 137) found that "socialization for storytelling in the Jewish-American families relies heavily on adult-child engagement in narrative events focused on child tellers (and protagonists); by contrast, in the Israeli families adults take up a larger proportion of narrative space, and hence socialization for narrative skills . . . relies more heavily on modeling and on allowing (limited) participation in adult-focused stories."

Even when they are not the primary authors, animators, or principals of mealtime narratives, this genre of communication constitutes a universal, powerful medium for socializing children into moral perspectives. Below, we consider how narrative practices recruit children into morally preferred ways of thinking, feeling, and acting in the world.

In the United States, dinner is often the moment of the day when family members reunite after work and school and is a cultural site for recounting incidents that transpired in the course of the day or the recent past. Telling such narratives often appears to be motivated by a desire not only to update others but also to solicit their sympathies for the teller's moral stance. A study of U.S. middle-class European American families (Ochs et al., 1989) found that family members frequently positioned themselves as morally superior to others (the "looking good" principle). In the excerpt below, the mother aligns with her daughter Lucy's self-righteous attitude about the punishment appropriate for a classmate's transgression. In recounting that the school principal (Mrs. Arnold) gave only one day of detention to a girl who pulled up another girl's skirt on the playground, Lucy begins her narrative with a clear moral framing (p. 244):

LUCY: I don't think Mrs. Arnold is being fair because . . . when we were back in school um—this girl—she pulled Valerie's dress up to here (*gestures with hand across chest*) in front of the boys.
MOTHER: Mhm?
LUCY: She only—all she did was get a day in detention.
MOTHER: Mhm? You think she should have gotten suspended? (*pause*)
LUCY: At least—that's—
MOTHER: Mhm?
LUCY: Not allowed in school.

Lucy's mother signals her willingness to go along with her daughter's indignation by voicing what Lucy would prefer as punishment for the transgression: suspension from school. After a detached, ironic commentary by Lucy's father ("Fortunately, capital punishment is still beyond the reach of elementary school principals"), both her mother and her little brother, Chuck, display rousing support for Lucy's position (p. 245):

MOTHER: Lucy was *really* embarrassed . . . I mean you really would have liked to kill the girl—huh? Cuz you were upset with her? But you were held back because you thought your school was going to do it and the school didn't do it and you feel upset.
(*pause*)
CHUCK: I think she should be in there for a *whole* MONTH or so well maybe (*pause*) *each day* she have to go there—*each* day *each* day . . .

Through this narrative interaction, Lucy becomes assured that she can count on the support of at least some of her family and that her mother knows her sentiments so well that she can elaborately voice them. Lucy's younger brother as well evidences that he has learned how to align with the majority family stance.

But there is a twist to this narrative interaction, which reveals the complexities of moral socialization at family mealtimes. Perhaps intentionally or perhaps unwittingly, young Chuck reveals that Lucy herself was given one day's detention the year before:

CHUCK: Lucy—you only went to it *once*—right?

Lucy's moral high ground is undermined by this disclosure. Her indignation turns out to be rooted in the fact that she and the classmate received the same amount of detention. We suggest that like Lucy, other children at U.S. dinner tables learn that it is sometimes difficult to look good when there are skeletons in your closet about which family members know.

Indeed, U.S. children often have difficulty garnering and maintaining their moral credibility when parents and siblings begin to probe their role in a narrated episode. Mealtimes in many U.S. and other households turn out to be cultural sites for surveillance not only of children's here-and-now comportment at the table, but also of their past and projected activities as narrated during mealtimes. As such, some children come to regard dinnertime as a provocative, even unpleasant moment when they are subjected to interrogation and criticism (Blum-Kulka, 1997; Ochs & Taylor, 1992; Taylor, 1995).

In Italian family dinnertimes, in contrast, parents almost always side with their children or position them as justified in their actions (Sterponi, 2002), as in the excerpt below (Sterponi, 2003, p. 91):

PAPÀ: Leonardo.
(*Leonardo looks at Papà*)
PAPÀ: Ascolta una cosa. [Listen to this.] Come mai oggi hai graffiato a Ivan tu? [How come *you* scratched Ivan today?]
(2.5) (*Leonardo looks at Papà*)
PAPÀ: Eh?
(1.0)
Come mai? Che t'aveva fato Ivan?
[How come? What had Ivan been doing to you?]

Here the father offers the possibility that Leonardo may have been defending himself rather than wantonly aggressive. In other Italian dinnertime narratives, a parent may take the blame himself or herself for a child's apparent misdemeanor.

Conclusion

This chapter has considered language socialization and cultural apprenticeship into family mealtimes. Ethnographic evidence from various parts of the world supports the notion that food and eating are not just biologically significant for the reproduction of families and social groups, but are saturated with social import. What constitutes mealtime comportment, for example, varies within and across communities, including the sequential ordering of who eats before, after, or along with whom; the social distribution of food; and the communicative roles expected of different mealtime participants. In many communities, children are often expected to eat after adults and to be relatively silent. Through engagement in this mealtime structure, children learn their lower social position relative to others. By contrast, in many households in the United States, children are expected to eat together with the adult members of their household and to vocally contribute to mealtime discourse. This mealtime structure promotes a more egalitarian ideology. Such egalitarianism may be contradicted, however, by a focus in many U.S. family mealtime discussions on parental attempts to control their children's past, present, and projected behavior through assessments and directives.

In addition, children are socialized into culturally divergent symbolic, moral, and emotional meanings associated with food and eating. At the dinner table of many U.S. families, for example, the dominant message is that children should eat their meal because it is good for their health, that is, it is nutritious. Alternatively, Italian families emphasize the pleasurable qualities of the meal they are consuming together. Because food is saturated with emotional meanings, children across many of the world's communities use it as a medium of resistance, including habitually refusing food as an extreme form of social control.

Meals are cultural sites where members of different generations and genders come to learn, reinforce, undermine, or transform each other's ways of acting, thinking, and feeling in the world, sometimes through cajoling, begging, probing, praising, bargaining, directing, ignoring, or otherwise interacting with one another in the course of nourishing one's body. These practices orient children both to mealtime comportment and to more encompassing dispositions expected of socially differentiated members. Though accentuated at feasts and ritual occasions, cultural apprenticeship and language socialization actually accrue and are given shape in the give and take of everyday mealtime interactions.

References

Anderson-Fye, E., & Becker, A. (2003). Socio-cultural aspects of eating disorders. In J. K. Thompson (Ed.), *The handbook of eating disorders and obesity* (pp. 565–589). Hoboken, NJ: Wiley.

Bloch, M. (1985). Almost eating the ancestors. *Man, 20*(4), 631–646.

Blum-Kulka, S. (1997). *Dinner talk: Cultural patterns of sociability and socialization in family discourse.* Mahwah, NJ: Erlbaum.

Bordo, S. (1993). *Unbearable weight: Feminism, Western culture, and the body.* Berkeley: University of California Press.

Bourdieu, P. (1977). *Outline of a theory of practice* (R. Nice, Trans.). Cambridge: Cambridge University Press.

Bourdieu, P. (1984). *Distinction: A social critique of the judgment of taste.* Cambridge, MA: Harvard University Press.

Bourdieu, P. (1990a). *In other words: Essays towards a reflexive sociology* (M. Adamson, Trans.). Palo Alto, CA: Stanford University Press.

Bourdieu, P. (1990b). *The logic of practice* (R. Nice, Trans.). Palo Alto, CA: Stanford University Press.

Capps, L., & Ochs, E. (2002). Cultivating prayer. In C. Ford, B. Fox, & S. Thompson (Eds.), *The language of turn and sequence* (pp. 39–55). New York: Oxford University Press.

Cole, M., & Cole, S. (1996). *The development of children.* New York: Freeman.

Cooper, E. (1986). Chinese table manners: You are how you eat. *Human Organization, 45*(2), 179–184.

De Geer, B. (2004). "Don't say it's disgusting!" Comments on socio-moral behavior in Swedish families. *Journal of Pragmatics, 36,* 1705–1725.

Douglas, M. (1975). *Deciphering a meal. Implicit meanings: Essays in anthropology.* New York: Routledge.

Dreyer, C. A., & Dreyer, A. S. (1973). Family dinner as a unique behavior habitat. *Family Processes, 12,* 291–301.

Eagleton, T. (2000). *The idea of culture.* Oxford: Blackwell.

Elias, N. (2000). *The civilizing process.* Oxford: Blackwell. (Original work published 1939.)

Farb, P., & Armelagos, G. (1980). *Consuming passions: The anthropology of eating.* Boston: Houghton Mifflin.

Feeley-Harnik, G. (1994). *The Lord's table: The meaning of food in early Judaism and Christianity.* Washington, DC: Smithsonian Institution Press.

Garfinkel, H. (1967). *Studies in ethnomethodology.* Upper Saddle River, NJ: Prentice Hall.

Garrett, P., & Baquedano-Lopez, P. (2002). Language socialization: Reproduction and continuity, transformation and change. *Annual Review of Anthropology, 31,* 339–361.

Geertz, C. (1973). *The interpretation of cultures.* New York: Basic Books.

Goffman, E. (1981). *Forms of talk.* Philadelphia: University of Pennsylvania Press.

Goody, J. (1982). *Cooking, cuisine, and class.* Cambridge: Cambridge University Press.

Gremillion, H. (2003). *Feeding anorexia: Gender and power at a treatment center.* Durham, NC: Duke University Press.

Hollan, D., & Wellenkamp, J. (1996). *The thread of life: Toraja reflections on the life cycle.* Honolulu: University of Hawaii Press.

Hsu, F., & Hsu, V. (1977). Modern China: North. In K. C. Chang (Ed.), *Food in Chinese culture* (pp. 295–316). New Haven, CT: Yale University Press.

Izquierdo, C. (2001). Betwixt and between: Seeking cure and meaning among the Matsigenka of the Peruvian Amazon. Unpublished doctoral dissertation, University of California, Los Angeles.

Izquierdo, C., & Paugh, A. (2003). Modeling, negotiating, fixing: Discourses of health among working families in Los Angeles. Unpublished manuscript, Los Angeles.

Katzman, M., & Lee, S. (1997). Beyond body image: The integration of feminist and transcultural theories in the understanding of self starvation. *International Journal of Eating Disorders, 22*(4), 385–394.

Kulick, D., & Schieffelin, B. B. (2004). Language socialization. In A. Duranti (Ed.), *A companion to linguistic anthropology* (pp. 349–368). Malden, MA: Blackwell.

Lacey, W. K. (1968). *The family in classical Greece.* Ithaca, NY: Cornell University Press.

Lave, J., & Wenger, E. (1991). *Situated learning: Legitimate peripheral participation.* Cambridge: Cambridge University Press.

LeVine, R. A. (1999). An agenda for psychological anthropology. *Ethos, 27*(1), 15–24.

Mead, G. H. (1934). *Mind, self, and society.* Chicago: University of Chicago Press.

Mintz, S., & Du Bois, C. (2002). The anthropology of food and eating. *Annual Review of Anthropology, 31,* 99–119.

Murcott, A. (1982). On the social significance of the "cooked dinner" in South Wales. *Anthropology of Food, 21*(4/5), 677–696.

Ochs, E. (1988). *Culture and language development: Language acquisition and language socialization in a Samoan village.* Cambridge: Cambridge University Press.

Ochs, E., & Capps, L. (2001). *Living narrative: Creating lives in everyday storytelling.* Cambridge, MA: Harvard University Press.

Ochs, E., Pontecorvo, C., & Fasulo, A. (1996). Socializing taste. *Ethnos, 6*(1), 7–46.

Ochs, E., & Schieffelin, B. B. (1984). Language acquisition and socialization: Three developmental stories. In R. A. Shweder & R. A. LeVine (Eds.), *Culture theory: Essay on mind, self, and emotion* (pp. 276–320). Cambridge: Cambridge University Press.

Ochs, E., & Schieffelin, B. B. (1995). The impact of language socialization on grammatical development. In P. Fletcher & B. MacWhinney (Eds.), *The handbook of child language* (pp. 73–94). Oxford: Blackwell.

Ochs, E., Smith, R., & Taylor, C. (1989). Detective stories at dinnertime: Problem-solving through co-narration. *Cultural Dynamics, 2,* 238–257.

Ochs, E., & Taylor, C. (1992). Family narrative as political activity. *Discourse and Society, 3*(3), 301–340.

Rogoff, B. (1990). *Apprenticeship in thinking.* New York: Oxford University Press.

Rogoff, B. (2003). *The cultural nature of human development.* New York: Oxford University Press.

Rubinstein, D. H. (1979). An ethnography of Micronesian childhood: Contexts of socialization on Fais Island. Unpublished doctoral dissertation, Stanford University.

Rydstrom, H. (2003). *Embodying morality: Growing up in rural Northern Vietnam.* Honolulu: University of Hawaii Press.

Sapir, E. (1993). *The psychology of culture: A course of lectures.* Reconstructed and edited by Judith T. Irvine. Berlin: Mouton de Gruyter.

Schieffelin, B. B. (1990). *The give and take of everyday life: Language socialization of Kaluli children.* Cambridge: Cambridge University Press.

Shohet, M. (2004). Narrating anorexia: Genres of recovery. Unpublished master's thesis, University of California, Los Angeles.

Sterponi, L. (2002). La costruzione discorsiva del posizionamento morale attraverso l'attivita del 'render conto' [The discursive construction of moral positioning through the activity of accountability]. Unpublished doctoral dissertation, University of Rome-La Sapienza.

Sterponi, L. (2003). Account episodes in family discourse: The making of morality in everyday interaction. *Discourse Studies, 5*(1), 79–100.

Taylor, C. E. (1995). Child as apprentice-narrator: Socializing voice, face, identity, and self-esteem amid the narrative politics of family dinner. Unpublished doctoral dissertation, University of Southern California.

Watson, J. (1987). From the common pot: Feasting with equals in Chinese society. *Anthropos, 82,* 389–401.

ELINOR OCHS is Distinguished Professor of Anthropology and Applied Linguistics at the University of California, Los Angeles, and director of the UCLA Sloan Center on Everyday Lives of Families.

MERAV SHOHET is a graduate student specializing in linguistic and psychocultural anthropology at the University of California, Los Angeles.

NEW DIRECTIONS FOR CHILD AND ADOLESCENT DEVELOPMENT • DOI 10.1002/cad

4

Participation in dinner table conversations offers children opportunities to acquire vocabulary, practice producing and understanding stories and explanations, acquire general knowledge, and learn how to talk in culturally appropriate ways.

Mealtime Talk That Supports Literacy Development

Catherine E. Snow, Diane E. Beals

It is not intuitively obvious that mealtimes can help children do well in school. We have all heard that breakfast is "a child's most important meal of the day," because its nutrition provides energy for learning. But family mealtimes can also contribute to children's linguistic and cognitive development in ways that support their learning to read and write. Take, for example, the conversation in five-year-old Rosalyn's family during dinner one evening:

FATHER: Pretty soon you'll be big enough to drive to the store and buy the groceries for us.
ROSALYN: I will?
MOTHER: (*laughs*)
FATHER: Well, about thirteen or fourteen years.
ROSALYN: I will?
FATHER: Sure. In fourteen years.
ROSALYN: That's fun.
FATHER: In fourteen years you'll be seventeen. And you'll have your driver's license and go grocery shopping.
MOTHER: In fourteen years, she'll be nineteen.
FATHER: Oh, right, I'm sorry. Gee! Only twelve years and you'll be seventeen. Suppose Cheryl (Rosalyn's older sister) will go grocery shopping for us when she gets her license?

NEW DIRECTIONS FOR CHILD AND ADOLESCENT DEVELOPMENT, no. 111, Spring 2006 © Wiley Periodicals, Inc.
Published online in Wiley InterScience (www.interscience.wiley.com) • DOI: 10.1002/cad.154

ROSALYN: Hmm (*laughs*).
FATHER: Maybe she'll offer to do it just so she can drive the car (*laughing*).
MOTHER: I don't know.
FATHER: That would be the only reason she'd offer.
MOTHER: Mmhm.
ROSALYN: That would be real good. (*giggles*). I hope she doesn't crash.
FATHER: Well, we hope she doesn't crash either.

In this segment of a longer mealtime conversation, Rosalyn is getting practice in making future plans and describing those plans to others. This is a form of narrative talk that helps children with school tasks such as recognizing sequences of events or planning to complete projects on time. Rosalyn also hears arithmetic talk—calculations of number of years until she is seventeen—and an implied explanation that one must be seventeen (or some advanced age) to drive legally. She is also exposed to a vocabulary word that many five year olds do not know: *license.* Her father does not stop to define the *license,* but the conversation gives Rosalyn some sense of the word's meaning—that you cannot drive without it and that you can get it only when you are older. All of this potential for learning occurs in a natural conversation engaged in for amusement by people who care about each other.

In this chapter, we argue that understanding how to promote language development in young children is of particular importance, not just because language skills are valued on their own but also because children's language skills are closely related to their literacy development. Literacy skills are a key contributor to successful academic outcomes such as on-time progress through the grades, high school graduation, and good performance on college entrance exams and other important educational assessments. We present evidence that family mealtimes can be a powerful site for children's language development.

Since the 1970s, family mealtimes have been extensively studied by researchers interested in child language development and parent-child interaction. The results of these studies have provided a rich portrait of how family members talk to each other in ways that help children learn the social rules and functions of talk.

Considerable information has emerged from these studies—for example:

- Mealtimes vary widely across social classes and race in amount and style of talk (Hall, Nagy, & Linn, 1984).
- Mealtime talk often incorporates discussions and explanations of current events, world knowledge, and even abstract general principles, not just in middle-class families (Davidson & Snow, 1995, 1996; Perlmann, 1984) but also in working-class families (Beals, 1993).

- Mealtime talk constitutes an opportunity for the problems of everyday life and proposed solutions to be discussed, often in the context of stories (Ochs, Taylor, Rudolph, & Smith, 1992).
- The ways in which families construct and develop their narratives vary as a function of culture (Aukrust, 2002; Aukrust & Snow, 1998; Blum-Kulka, 1993; Blum-Kulka & Snow, 1992).
- Mealtime conversations constitute a key locus for immigrant families' efforts to reinforce the home language, but also for children to negotiate control over familial language use (Pan, 1995).
- The distribution of mealtime talk over the two languages of bilingual families relates to children's proficiency in those two languages (Kasuya, 2002; Pan, 1995).
- Even in cultures in which a high level of formal politeness is the rule, family talk at mealtimes tends to be fairly direct and hardly ever characterized by extremely polite indirectness (Blum-Kulka, 1994, 1997).
- Nonetheless, dinner table conversations constitute an opportunity for explicitly teaching aspects of politeness ranging from not talking with one's mouth full to not interrupting to using *please* and *thank you* (Becker, 1990; Gleason, Perlmann, & Greif, 1984; Snow, Perlmann, Gleason, & Hooshyar, 1990).

In sum, these studies have demonstrated that mealtimes are one locus of children's experience with language and its social uses (Pan, Perlmann, & Snow, 2000). They learn what appropriate topics are, how to stay on topic, how to give enough information to the listener, and what the socially acceptable means of communication are.

The studies point to the ways that mealtime research has contributed to our understanding of child language development. In this chapter, we focus on how mealtime talk can contribute to children's success in school and how later school success relates to the language skills that can be acquired during mealtime conversations.

Features of Family Mealtimes That Contribute to Language Development and School Success

A number of features of family mealtimes create opportunities for children to acquire language skills relevant to academic success. Many forms of family interaction other than mealtime talk contribute to children's language: engaging in fantasy play with toddlers, reading books with children starting in infancy and continuing through the early school years, talking to children while chauffeuring them about, and many other conversational interactions can all contribute to child language outcomes (Dickinson & Tabors, 2001). However, we argue that mealtimes offer particular affordances, *or opportunities to learn,* that in some families may be less likely to occur in other settings.

NEW DIRECTIONS FOR CHILD AND ADOLESCENT DEVELOPMENT • DOI 10.1002/cad

These unique affordances include the availability of extended discourse, which we define as talk centered on a particular topic that extends over several utterances or conversational turns. The extended discourse we have studied mostly falls into two kinds: explanatory talk and narrative talk (Beals & Snow, 1994; Snow & Kurland, 1996). Explanations can be initiated by genuine child questions (for example, "Mommy, what does 'budget' mean?") or by parents trying to ensure their children understand something (for example, "So why do you think the firemen carry oxygen tanks with them?"). Explanatory talk brings with it the introduction of sophisticated, nonpresent topics and the opportunity to learn about the world (Beals, 1993).

Mealtime narratives, in contrast, often emerge as part of catching-up talk—in response, for example, to questions like, "What happened at preschool today?" Narratives are often about relatively familiar topics but may require the use of complex language structures, for example, to keep track of who is who and what happened when in the stories being told. And they can be opportunities for considering hypotheticals or conditionals (for example, "Let's consider why that made your sister mad at you"), which introduce complex language forms.

In addition to offering opportunities for extended discourse, mealtime talk often introduces relatively sophisticated vocabulary, typically in the middle of narrative or explanatory discourse. Knowing sophisticated words like *budget, oxygen,* and *consider* becomes important to children's success in participating in classroom talk and reading after grade 3.

Mealtimes as a Site for Extended Discourse

Talk is organized into structured units at many levels. Words are one such level: pronouncing a word correctly and using it meaningfully requires a lot of knowledge about it. Sentences (or, more properly, utterances) are another such level, and producing meaningful and grammatically correct utterances requires a lot of knowledge about how language works. In addition to learning words and learning to construct grammatical utterances, children need to master two additional levels of structure: the conversational turn, which is often made up of several related utterances, and extended discourse, which can encompass more than one conversational turn and may be constructed by two or more speakers collaboratively.

Data from the Home-School Study of Language and Literacy Development (Dickinson & Tabors, 2001; Snow, 1991) suggest that dinner table conversations offer rich opportunities for extended discourse, in part because talk is (at least in the families we studied) part of what is meant to happen at the dinner table. In other words, these families shared a cultural norm that mealtimes are family time, that mealtimes last more than just a few minutes, that pleasant conversation involving all the family members is appropriate, that all the family members should be present, and that every member of the family should contribute to the conversation. These norms were embraced by low-income families with low parental educational levels participating in the Home-School Study, as well as by middle-class families in other studies (Blum-Kulka, 1997). Of course, neither low-income nor middle-income families behave in accordance with these norms all the time, but they do (with a few exceptions) demonstrate their knowledge and acceptance of them.

Dinner table conversations are used in the families we and others have studied as opportunities to catch up on the day's events, plan the next day's activities, reminisce about shared experiences, answer puzzling questions, seek explanations for strange happenings, and solve problems. The conversations that fulfill these varied functions share certain characteristics. First, they are centered around a single topic. Second, the topic is complex enough that the talk goes on for several utterances or turns. Third, to be fully explored, the topic often needs input from several participants—in other words, it becomes a multiparty discourse. These various features mean that the talk is likely to be linguistically complex, cognitively challenging, highly engaging, and thus the perfect opportunity for children to gain language skills (Snow & Blum-Kulka, 2002). Consider the following example of three-year-old Tommy retelling a particularly vivid dream and discussing with his mother which parts of it were and were not real (in these transcribed examples, xxx is used to indicate some talk that is not comprehensible):

MOTHER: There aren't a real lot of wild animals here.
TOMMY: No, but if we see a whole bunch um I would
waked up. And when I waked up they will still be there.
MOTHER: Think so?
TOMMY: Mmhm. Because I see them when I'm asleep, when I was asleep,
    I, my dreams xxx.
MOTHER: Yeah. When you're asleep sometimes your dreams are very real.
    But it's just your imagination working while the rest of you sleeps.
TOMMY: Mommy, Mommy? My dreams did come true.
MOTHER: No?
TOMMY: It did.
MOTHER: It did? What was your dream about?
TOMMY: It was a monster and I was xxx with his tongue it, Mom, his, his
    whole xxx and he dropped me on my neck.
MOTHER: The monster grabbed you on your head but that didn't come
    true. No monster really grabbed you on your neck.
TOMMY: It did come true.
MOTHER: It did? When?
TOMMY: A long time ago.
MOTHER: Yeah?
TOMMY: And it jabbed me in the eye.
MOTHER: No, honey, it didn't come true.

NEW DIRECTIONS FOR CHILD AND ADOLESCENT DEVELOPMENT • DOI 10.1002/cad

TOMMY: Mmhm.

MOTHER: You know I would never let any monsters get you. Besides what did I tell you about monsters?

TOMMY: What?

MOTHER: They're only make-believe and they only live in movies because somebody with a wonderful imagination makes up monsters. And all other sort of special effects to make the really scary monsters, you know, like how you watch Michael Jackson? And they show him putting his makeup on for "Thriller"? That's just because somebody had a great imagination.

TOMMY Mmhm.

MOTHER: But no there's no such things as monsters.

Explanatory Talk. This example displays characteristics of explanatory talk that are directly relevant to its value in promoting children's language development. First, explanatory and narrative talk are somewhat mingled together here. The conversation starts as an explanation about the propinquity of wild animals, segues into a personal narrative about a dream, then again becomes a multifaceted explanation, highlighting both the unreality of monsters and the protection available from mothers. This mixture of narrative and explanatory talk is quite common in conversation.

Second, this stretch of talk deals with complex issues and is richly informative: What is real and what is not? Can we believe what happens in our dreams? How is the appearance of monsters created? Why do monsters in dreams seem so real? In the process of providing answers to questions like these, parents are, in effect, explaining the world to their children.

Third, the talk is co-constructed. In other words, both Tommy and his mother contribute to the production of a coherent stretch of talk, and both of their contributions are crucial to the shape of the discourse that emerges.

Fourth, relatively low-frequency, sophisticated vocabulary words occur in the course of this conversation: *imagination, special effects, jabbed.* Such terms are much less likely to occur in brief exchanges, as it is the development of the topic that makes them necessary. Compare this long segment to the kind of mealtime talk designed to manage the meal: for example, "Eat your peas," "I want more noodles," "Where's the milk?" "I dropped my fork") or the behavior of the diners ("Sit up straight," "Stop kicking your sister," "Where's your napkin?"). Such management talk rarely extends beyond a single conversational turn and almost never includes rare words or nominates complicated topics.

Unlike management talk, which is ubiquitous, the amount of explanatory talk varies across families (and across cultures). Though, on average, thirteen to fourteen explanations (about 15 percent of all talk) occurred in the mealtime conversations of low-income American families with preschool-aged children (Beals & Snow, 1994), some families did none of it and some did much more.

Narrative Talk. Narrative talk recounts past events or plans future events. Blum-Kulka (1993, 1997) has shown that American middle-class families' dinner table conversations often follow the implicit rule that everyone present has the right to "tell about his/her day." In one such family conversation, for example, the five-year-old child had been inadvertently ignored, but asserted her rights by insisting, "Mommy, who will I tell my day to?"

Narrative talk, like explanatory talk, offers opportunities for complex language, the transmission of information about the world, and sophisticated vocabulary. Consider the following narrative sequence from a low-income family's dinner table conversation, in which five-year-old Astra and her mother talk at length about her day at school and another child's moral transgressions:

MOTHER: What Miss Connie say today?
ASTRA: Uh . . .
MOTHER: Freddie was good in the class?
ASTRA: He say no to Miss Connie when she, when she when she told him to do his homework.
MOTHER: Really?
ASTRA: Yeah.
MOTHER So what she said to him?
ASTRA: He went down to the principal's office.

This narrative was possible because Astra's mother worked hard to elicit it, using her knowledge that Freddie was a likely source of "tellable" events, and posing questions to specify the chronological and logical sequence.

Low-income American families devote about as much mealtime talk to narratives as to explanations (about 15 percent of utterances). But narratives are typically longer, so only three or four get told on average (data collection and analysis are described later; Beals & Snow, 1994). Again, though, some families do no narrating, and some do a quite a lot.

Furthermore, the frequency, length, and kind of narratives and explanations produced at the dinner table vary across cultures, across language groups, and as a function of social class. Comparing American families with Norwegian families of similar social class, we found that the American families produced less narrative talk than the Norwegians (16 percent versus 31 percent of utterances) and more explanatory talk (22 percent versus 12 percent of utterances). Even the youngest children in the two groups of families fit the pattern; Norwegian preschoolers asked more questions that evoked narrative responses, whereas American preschoolers asked more often for explanations (Aukrust & Snow, 1998).

Furthermore, the narratives told at American dinner tables recounted events that were more surprising and out of the ordinary than the Norwegian narratives. It seemed as if the cultural rules defining what is worth telling were quite different, with rather minor deviations from normalcy (for example, "Nils wore a green sweater to preschool") sufficient to warrant reports in Norway, but only rather more dramatic events ("Johnny threw up and it was orange") meriting the conversational floor at American mealtimes (Aukrust, 2002; Aukrust & Snow, 1998).

Israeli dinner table conversations are much more likely to feature narratives that involve reminiscing (for example, "Let's see if we can remember all the pets we've had") or retelling of events in which all the family members present had actually participated than in the conversations of American Jewish families of matched social class. American Jewish families, like all other American families, seem to prefer stories about events that are new to at least one member of the audience—for example, "Tell Daddy about what you saw at the playground this afternoon!" (Blum-Kulka, 1997).

Thus, in addition to providing opportunities for children to hear and participate in using complex language and acquire new information, extended discourse at the dinner table may also represent a powerful, though subtle, way of inducting children into the rules of talk typical of their culture. In order to be a linguistically proficient Norwegian, it is important to know that stories are valued over explanations and that one should notice modest violations of the social norms because those are the substance of good stories. To be a successful American conversationalist, one needs to know that stories should be splashy and dramatic and that they have to be told in a way that is understandable to an audience that knows nothing about the event itself. To be a successful Israeli dinner companion, one needs to be able to reconstruct with other participants stories about familiar events in ways that keep them interesting to all involved. The specifics of how to be a charming companion are quite particular to each of these cultures.

Connections Between Literacy Development and Dinner Table Conversations

Children can and do learn a lot from listening, watching, and participating in multiparty conversations with their families (Snow & Blum-Kulka, 2002). As such, mealtime conversations constitute an important place to study the connections between a family's ways of talking during the preschool years and their children's developing oral language and literacy abilities.

In this section, we describe the Home-School Study of Language and Literacy Development, a major longitudinal study that traced the links between eighty-three children's oral language experiences in their preschool years and their literacy skills through grade school and high school (Dickinson & Tabors, 2001; Snow, 1991). The data collected in this study provide powerful portraits of styles of individual family interaction that result in varying levels of literacy development and subsequent school success.

New Directions for Child and Adolescent Development • DOI 10.1002/cad

Data Collection. One major assumption of the Home-School Study was that different social interaction settings provide different affordances for learning language and literacy, so data collection was wide ranging. A home visitor recorded conversations between mothers and their children at ages three, four, and five while they played together with a set of toys and read a book. At the end of the visit, the researcher left a blank audiotape and recorder and asked the mother to record a typical family mealtime. The mealtimes were recorded without the home visitor present. The tape and recorder were collected at a later date.

Each year, some of the families failed to follow through on recording a mealtime; however, we collected sixty-four tapes when the children were three years old, forty-five at age four, and fifty-one at age five from the sixty-eight families remaining. Thus, 160 mealtime conversations were taped, from sixty-eight different families (with seventy different focus children, since two families had twins).

The families participating in the Home-School Study were English-speaking, low-income families living in the greater Boston area. About one-third were African American or Hispanic, and the remainder were white.

Mealtime talk usually involved more than just the mother and target child; some families had siblings or other children present. Fathers were present in 52 of the 160 mealtimes, and other adults (uncles, grandparents, family friends) also participated. Mothers and children together accounted for approximately three-quarters of the talk. Fathers, even when present, contributed relatively little to the conversations.

Mealtime conversations varied enormously in character across the families. They ranged in length from two to forty-seven minutes, averaging about twenty minutes. Most mealtimes consisted of family members meeting in one place at the same time, although one consisted of two children eating cereal in front of the television, while another "mealtime" was in fact a play-by-play description of mother and child making cornbread; the mother reported that since she and her son live alone, there is no formal mealtime. Nonetheless, most of the recordings were an evening meal in which interaction among family members was a priority. In a few, the television was a focus of attention.

What the mothers thought we expected from the mealtime recording is important to consider. Mothers were aware that we were studying their child's language and, because they were asked to place the tape recorder near the child in the study, often concluded that we wanted talk from that child. Therefore, most tended to make a concerted effort to draw that child into the conversation. Some mothers took the recording when the target child was three years old to be some kind of performance and in a few cases asked children to recite their ABC's, count, or sing a favorite song. This kind of performance was much less frequent in the age-four and age-five home

NEW DIRECTIONS FOR CHILD AND ADOLESCENT DEVELOPMENT • DOI 10.1002/cad

visits, perhaps due to the children's enhanced ability to initiate and join in the family's conversations.

As the children moved through their school years, their developing language and literacy abilities were tested at regular intervals. Tests included (among many others; see Dickinson & Tabors, 2001) the Peabody Picture Vocabulary Test (PPVT-R), which measures a child's receptive vocabulary, and a formal definitions task, a measure of a child's expressive vocabulary. We focus on these measures here for two reasons: use of rare vocabulary is a major feature of extended discourse, and vocabulary knowledge is one of the most powerful predictors of reading abilities (Anderson & Freebody, 1981). In addition, we examined children's reading achievement on the reading portion of the Wide Range Achievement Test (WRAT), administered in the second grade.

Explanatory and Narrative Talk as Predictors. As we saw earlier, explanatory and narrative talk each accounted for approximately 15 percent of the mealtime talk in the Home-School Study, but there was a wide variation in how much families engaged in such talk. We found that children's exposure to extended discourse was associated with their later vocabulary and reading achievement scores. In correlational analyses, Beals (1991) found that that the proportion of mealtime talk devoted to narratives was weakly but positively associated with the ability to give formal definitions (expressive vocabulary) ($r = .293, p = .062$). In addition, percentage of narrative talk at age five was correlated positively with the PPVT (receptive vocabulary) in grade 6 ($r = .317, p = .045$) six years later. Furthermore, children's exposure to narrative talk at age three was related to reading achievement (WRAT Reading) scores in grade 2 ($r = .338, p = .058$).

Exposure to explanatory talk also predicted PPVT scores. Percentage of explanatory talk at age four was moderately and positively correlated with PPVT scores in grades 6 ($r = .404, p = .018$) and 7 ($r = .371, p = .033$). These findings suggest that explanatory talk provides substantial support for word learning.

These links between a child's exposure to extended discourse in mealtimes and much later vocabulary scores point to the special affordances of mealtimes in providing opportunities for learning new words and concepts. What exactly are the features of extended discourse that create these affordances?

Rare Words. Topics that bring required sophisticated vocabulary and introduce interesting concepts are potent sources for children's word learning. A major affordance created by the commitment to extended talk at the dinner table is thus exposure to sophisticated vocabulary.

Rosalyn's parents in the first example in the chapter used the word *license* incidentally in a way that allowed some initial inference about what a license is. However, parents could discuss interesting topics using sophisticated words, but employ those words in ways that reveal little about their meanings.

In a study of the same mealtime conversations described above, Beals (1997) identified each use of a rare word. Rare words were defined as words not found on the 3,000 Most Common Words List (Chall & Dale, 1995). Each rare word use was coded to reflect whether and how a child could learn something about the word's meaning. For example, cases where the speaker physically pointed to a novel item or demonstrated an action were coded Physical Context. In the next example, the mother demonstrated the action of "twirling" and indicated a "cube," giving three-year-old Emily a chance to learn or confirm the meanings of these words:

EMILY: Me need butter on this!
FATHER: Yes you do need butter on that corn.
MOTHER: Yeah here's the butter you *twirl* it over the top of the big *cube* of butter.
EMILY: Oh.
MOTHER: Dad'll show you how.
EMILY: Me?
FATHER: Um I don't want your fingers all over it though.
FATHER: There we go.

Cases of the speaker identifying social norms or violations of norms were coded Social Context. In the next example, four-year-old Catherine's older brother, Robert, was called rude for humming and talking while eating.

BROTHER: (*humming and talking with food in his mouth*)
MOTHER: Robert.
SISTER: Ma can you please?
BROTHER: (*humming and talking with food in his mouth*)
MOTHER: Robert don't do that, that's *rude*.

Explaining a word by calling on past experiences or general knowledge was coded Prior Knowledge. In this example, three-year-old Tommy's mother reminded him of a trip to the park to elicit the word *iguana*:

MOTHER: Tommy you don't remember what you said you saw at the park?
TOMMY: Oh yeah.
MOTHER: What?
TOMMY: Um . . . . I don't know.
MOTHER: You don't remember the word?
TOMMY: No.
MOTHER: An *iguana*.
TOMMY: Oh an *iguana* xxx.
MOTHER: Yeah!

MOTHER: Did its owner let you pat him?
TOMMY: No.
MOTHER: Was he walking around all by himself?
TOMMY: Mmhm.

The fourth category, Semantic Support, in which a speaker gives some direct verbal semantic information, was an especially varied one. The next two examples demonstrate semantic support using somewhat different approaches. In the first example, the mother gives a definition of *cramps* at four-year-old George's request. In the next example, the mother juxtaposed *colander* to its synonym, drainer, while five-year-old Suzanne listened.

MOTHER: You have to wait a little while so you don't get *cramps*.
GEORGE: What's *cramps*?
MOTHER: *Cramps* are when your stomach feels all tight and it hurts 'cause you have food in it.
MOTHER: And you're in the water.
GRANDMA: Is this done? (*referring to noodles*)
MOTHER: Needs to be drained!
GRANDMA: Oh it needs to be drained in the xxx regular *drainer*?
MOTHER: *Colander* or just put the cover to the edge and drain the water out.

Informativeness of Rare Word Use. The 160 transcripts yielded 1,631 exchanges in which rare words were used, of which about two-thirds were informative. In 1,053 cases (or 64.6 percent), it was judged the child could learn something about the meaning of the word; 492 cases (30.1 percent) were coded as uninformative, and 86 (5.3 percent) were considered uncodable (due to unintelligible material in the transcript).

The most frequent support strategy used was semantic (see Table 4.1), accounting for 651 of 1,066 strategies used (some exchanges were double-coded). The physical context strategy was used 201 times, social context 140 times, and prior knowledge only 74 times. The physical context strategy would probably have appeared more often if food words had not been excluded from consideration.

The frequency of informative uses of rare words was positively correlated with both age five PPVT scores (age three, mealtime: $r = .417, p < .001$; age four: $r = .433, p < .005$; age 5: $r = .545, p < .001$) and age seven PPVTs (age three mealtime: $r = .368, p < .001$; age four: $r = .495, p < .001$; age five: $r = .518, p < .001$). The more often rare words were used in informative ways during the children's preschool mealtimes, the greater their vocabularies were at ages five and seven.

While use of each strategy was significantly correlated with later vocabulary scores, use of the semantic support strategy was most strongly related

Table 4.1. Types of Support to Vocabulary Learning

Age of Child	Number of Mealtimes	Semantic Support	Physical Context	Social Context	Prior Knowledge	Total
Three years	64	238	78	40	29	385
Four years	45	188	54	46	23	311
Five years	51	225	69	54	22	370
Total	160	651	201	140	74	1,066
Percentage		61	19	13	7	100

to PPVT at age five (age three mealtime: $r = .348$, $p < .01$; age four: $r = .481$, $p < .005$; age five: $r = .575$, $p < .001$) and age seven (age four mealtime: $r = .481$, $p < .005$; age five: $r = .500$, $p < .001$). Children's exposure during the preschool years to informative uses of rare words, and especially semantic support strategies, appears to create many opportunities for word learning.

The predictive power of rare word use highlights the importance of mealtime conversation as a source of vocabulary for young children. Mealtimes allow extended discourse, which generates occasions for rare words to be used in informative ways.

Relation to Literacy?

These findings demonstrate that the kind of talk that normally occurs at mealtimes provides rich information to children about the meanings of words, and thus constitutes a context for learning vocabulary embedded in all the other kinds of learning that are going on: learning to participate as a family member, learning to be a member of the larger culture, learning to give explanations and tell stories, learning to take turns, and learning to enjoy family interactions. Of course, we know from experimental studies that certain language contexts promote children's vocabulary learning. But this study confirms that relationship in natural interaction, demonstrating a link between the kinds of spontaneous, everyday conversations that are typical of mealtimes and children's learning of new words and what they mean, and thus demonstrating as well the potential of mealtimes to contribute to children's literacy and school success. Weizman and Snow (2001) showed that mealtime was a more richly supportive context for the use of rare words in informative contexts than toy play or even book reading.

It might seem surprising to suggest that conversations such as those we have excerpted here contribute to literacy success. Is reading books with children not the best way to promote literacy growth? Is not the essence of literacy knowing the alphabet, recognizing words, writing with correct spelling? Those skills are, of course, crucial to literacy development—but they are skills that can be acquired at school. Good readers can do many things beyond reading words: reading and understanding stories; reading to learn social studies, math, and science in the middle elementary grades; and writing stories and essays. Such abilities require a diverse set of abilities, including producing and comprehending extended discourse, knowing many words, and having knowledge about many topics. These are the skills that are built through interesting conversations. The examination of mealtime conversations in the Home-School Study has shown strong, positive relationships between specific kinds of talk at mealtimes during the preschool years and literacy measures when the child is older, a finding that has emerged from other studies as well (West, Stanovich, & Mitchell, 1993). The more children are exposed to extended discourse during mealtime conversations, the more chances they have to acquire vocabulary, understand stories and explanations, and know things about the world. Because these are capacities that are drawn on heavily in school but are not typically much attended to in preschool or primary classrooms, children who have had the chance to acquire them at home have an important advantage in pursuing academic success.

Future Research

While mealtimes have been extensively studied as a site for child language development and family interaction, the majority of those studies have been descriptive or correlational. Thus, while we argue for the likely impact of dinner table talk on children's language and literacy development, we would prefer a stronger basis for inferences linking dinner table talk causally to child outcomes.

Of course, it is hard to assign families randomly to groups that vary on frequency and length of family mealtimes. But it would be possible to incorporate taping, transcription, and discourse analytical procedures such as those exemplified in this chapter into evaluations of policies designed to promote family mealtimes, to see if such policies indeed improve the language environment of young children. It would also be possible to evaluate the effectiveness of parental education focused on techniques for promoting rich discourse at the dinner table. A model here is offered by the success of dialogic reading instruction in modifying adult interactive styles while reading books with their children (Whitehurst et al., 1988, 1994).

Another line of work that would be of particular importance given the increasing cultural diversity of U.S. society is to explore cultural variation in the use of mealtime as a place for conversation. The educator's goal is to promote the kind of talk that happens in many American families at dinner because it is associated with academic achievement and literacy outcomes; if that talk occurs in another setting for some immigrant groups, then it would be counterproductive to promote family mealtimes for those groups. We need to understand the dynamics of family talk specific to each of the many groups that make up U.S. society.

References

Anderson, R. C., & Freebody, P. (1981). Vocabulary knowledge. In J. T. Guthrie (Ed.), *Comprehension and teaching: Research reviews* (pp. 77–116). Newark, DE: International Reading Association.

Aukrust, V. G. (2002). "What did you do in school today?" Speech genres and tellability in multiparty family mealtime conversations in two cultures. In S. Blum-Kulka & C. E. Snow (Eds.), *Talking to adults* (pp. 55–84). Mahwah, NJ: Erlbaum.

Aukrust, V. G., & Snow, C. E. (1998). Narratives and explanations during mealtime conversations in Norway and the U.S. *Language in Society, 27,* 221–246.

Beals, D. E. (1991). "I know who makes ice cream": Explanations in mealtime conversations of low-income families of preschoolers. Unpublished doctoral dissertation, Harvard University.

Beals, D. E. (1993). Explanations in low-income families' mealtime conversations. *Applied Psycholinguistics, 14,* 489–513.

Beals, D. E. (1997). Sources of support for learning words in conversation: Evidence from mealtimes. *Journal of Child Language, 24*(3), 673–694.

Beals, D. E., & Snow, C. E. (1994). "Thunder is when the angels are upstairs bowling": Narratives and explanations at the dinner table. *Journal of Narrative and Life History, 4,* 331–352.

Becker, J. (1990). Processes in the acquisition of pragmatic competence. In G. Conti-Ramsden & C. E. Snow (Eds.), *Children's language* (pp. 7–24). Mahwah, NJ: Erlbaum.

Blum-Kulka, S. (1993). "You got to know how to tell a story": Telling, tales, and tellers in American and Israeli narrative events at dinner. *Language in Society, 22,* 361–402.

Blum-Kulka, S. (1994). The dynamics of family dinner-talk: Cultural contexts for children's passages to adult discourse. *Research on Language and Social Interaction, 27,* 1–51.

Blum-Kulka, S. (1997). *Dinner talk: Cultural patterns of sociability and socialization in family discourse.* Mahwah, NJ: Erlbaum.

Blum-Kulka, S., & Snow, C. E. (1992). Developing autonomy for tellers, tales, and telling in family narrative-events. *Journal of Narrative and Life History, 2,* 187–217.

Chall, J. S., & Dale, E. (1995). *Readability revisited: The New Dale-Chall readability formula.* Cambridge, MA: Brookline Books.

Davidson, R. G., & Snow, C. E. (1995). The linguistic environment of early readers. *Journal of Research in Childhood Education, 10,* 5–21.

Davidson, R. G., & Snow, C. E. (1996). Five-year-olds' interactions with fathers versus mothers. *First Language, 16,* 223–242.

Dickinson, D., & Tabors, P. (Eds.). (2001). *Beginning literacy with language: Young children learning at home and school.* Baltimore, MD: Brookes Publishing.

Gleason, J. B., Perlmann, R., & Greif, E. (1984). What's the magic word: Learning language through politeness routines. *Discourse Processes, 7,* 493–502.

Hall, W. S., Nagy, W. E., & Linn, R. (1984). *Spoken words: Effects of situation and social group on oral word usage and frequency.* Mahwah, NJ: Erlbaum.

Kasuya, H. (2002). Sociolinguistic aspects of language choice in English/Japanese bilingual children. In S. Blum-Kulka & C. E. Snow (Eds.), *Talking to adults* (pp. 15–32). Mahwah, NJ: Erlbaum.

Ochs, E., Taylor, C., Rudolph, D., & Smith, R. (1992). Storytelling as a theory-building activity. *Discourse Processes, 15,* 37–72.

Pan, B. A. (1995). Code negotiation in bilingual families: "My body starts speaking English." *Journal of Multilingual and Multicultural Development, 16,* 315–327.

Pan, B. A., Perlmann, R., & Snow, C. E. (2000). Food for thought: Dinner table as a context for observing parent-child discourse. In L. Menn & N. B. Ratner (Eds.), *Methods for studying language production* (pp. 205–224). Mahwah, NJ: Erlbaum.

Perlmann, R. (1984). Variations in socialization styles: Family talk at the dinner table. Unpublished doctoral dissertation, Boston University.

Snow, C. E. (1991). The theoretical basis for relationships between language and literacy in development. *Journal of Research in Childhood Education, 6,* 5–10.

Snow, C. E., & Blum-Kulka, S. (2002). From home to school: School-age children talking with adults. In S. Blum-Kulka & C. E. Snow (Eds.), *Talking to adults* (pp. 327–341). Mahwah, NJ: Erlbaum.

Snow, C. E., & Kurland, B. F. (1996). Sticking to the point: Talk about magnets as a context for engaging in scientific discourse. In D. Hicks (Ed.), *Child discourse and social learning: An interdisciplinary perspective.* Cambridge: Cambridge University Press.

Snow, C. E., Perlmann, R., Gleason, J. B., & Hooshyar, N. (1990). Developmental perspectives on politeness: Sources of children's knowledge. *Journal of Pragmatics, 14,* 289–305.

Weizman, Z., & Snow, C. E. (2001). Lexical input as related to children's vocabulary acquisition: Effects of sophisticated exposure and support for meaning. *Developmental Psychology, 37,* 265–279.

West, R. F., Stanovich, K. E., & Mitchell, H. R. (1993). Reading in the real world and its correlates. *Reading Research Quarterly, 28,* 34–50.

Whitehurst, G. J., Arnold, D. H., Epstein, J. N., Angell, A. L., Smith, M., & Fischel, J. E. (1994). A picture book reading intervention in daycare and home for children from low-income families. *Developmental Psychology, 30,* 679–689.

Whitehurst, G. J., Falco, F. L., Lonigan, C., Fischel, J. E., Valdez-Menchaca, M. C., DeBaryshe, B. D., & Caulfield, M. (1988). Accelerating language development through picture-book reading. *Developmental Psychology, 24,* 552–558.

CATHERINE E. SNOW is the Henry Lee Shattuck Professor of Education at the Harvard Graduate School of Education.

DIANE E. BEALS is an associate professor and director of the School of Education at the University of Tulsa.

5

This chapter focuses on how the routine elements of family mealtimes such as assigned tasks and the more emotional ritual aspects such as recognition of feelings are related to children's well-being and the creation of a family identity.

Routine and Ritual Elements in Family Mealtimes: Contexts for Child Well-Being and Family Identity

Barbara H. Fiese, Kimberly P. Foley, Mary Spagnola

"How was your day today?" "Who is going to pick the kids up from soccer tomorrow?" "I don't like my food touching!" These are common phrases heard at many dinner tables. There is a cadence to family mealtimes where a review of the day's activities is blended with plans for the future and sprinkled with jokes and nicknames only family members can understand. In this chapter, we focus on the routine elements of family mealtimes as well as the more emotional and affective aspects associated with family rituals. Both dimensions are proposed to be related to children's well-being and contribute to the creation of a family identity. We draw from the existing literature as well as transcripts of mealtime conversations collected through studies conducted at the Syracuse University Family Research Lab. Our purpose is to illustrate family mealtimes as multilayered activities that serve to regulate behavior and hold deep symbolic meaning for participants.

Child development researchers have long been interested in how families regulate behavior and socialize children into group mores. What makes the study of family mealtimes distinctive is its focus on everyday practices shared by multiple members of society, yet each family comes to carry out these tasks in its own unique way. For some families, mealtimes are highly

Preparation of this chapter was supported in part by a grant from the National Institute of Mental Health (MH 51771).

structured affairs with a set time to eat, clearly defined roles, a shared understanding of what topics are suitable for dinnertime conversations, and rules for when members can be excused from the table. For other families, there may be a more laissez-faire approach to collective gatherings with few expectations for attendance, random role assignment, or even few rules for expression of negative affect. Thus, there is the opportunity to consider variations in daily routine practices that may portend variations in child mental health.

Why might psychologists be interested in the study of family mealtimes? There are at least two answers to this question. First, the study of family mealtimes provides an opportunity to directly observe patterns of social interaction that have been found to be related to a variety of mental health outcomes in children. For example, when family members engage in more positive interaction patterns at the dinner table, their children are also less likely to express problematic behaviors in other settings (Dickstein, St. Andre, Sameroff, Seifer, & Schiller, 1999; Fiese & Marjinsky, 1999). This does not necessarily mean that negative interaction patterns at the dinner table cause problematic behaviors in children. Rather, interaction patterns we observe during a routine mealtime may be consistent with what we know about healthy family functioning. There is a long research tradition in developmental psychology that has documented the importance of warm, responsive, and sensitive interaction patterns in fostering more optimal child outcomes. Thus, mealtimes provide a window into significant patterns of social interaction. However, we extend previous work by considering how the family negotiates this face-to-face task of organizing the group while feeding individuals.

A second reason to study mealtimes is that they illustrate family identity and the creation of a sense of group membership. In this regard, gathering together at the table over time reflects how family members come to represent or understand what it means to be a member of this particular group. Mealtimes are replete with symbolism, ranging from the types of blessings said, foods served, and even how seats are assigned. The symbolic nature of family mealtimes contributes to family identities that can be supportive or exclusionary. Often these beliefs are grounded in practices that extend across two or more generations. Thus, we also consider how family mealtimes shape beliefs about relationships, which in turn affect child well-being.

We aim to place the study of mealtimes as both a context for understanding how group-level interaction patterns are related to child well-being as well as how these repetitive interactions come to form part of the symbolic foundation of family life. We have found that through the study of family routines and rituals, we can delve into the multiple layers of and meanings surrounding mealtimes. Let us first examine the distinctions between routines and rituals.

Family Routines and Rituals

Although *routine* and *ritual* are often used interchangeably, it is possible to distinguish between them. One of the reasons it is difficult to clearly define routines and rituals is that they typically mean something different for each family. Indeed, it is this personal nature of daily activities and unique celebrations that holds special significance for family mealtimes. For our purposes, it is important to make such a distinction because routines are typically directly observable and rituals are more closely linked to symbolic aspects of family life.

Routines and rituals can be distinguished along three dimensions: communication, commitment, and continuity (Fiese et al., 2002). Routine communications are typically direct and instrumental. The intent is to get something done, such as "get your elbows off the table," or to assign roles, such as "it's your turn to do the dishes tonight." Routine commitments focus on the task itself with very little afterthought about what happened during the meal once it is over. In terms of continuity, it is likely that seat assignments are the same from meal to meal, the reminder to say "please and thank you" is repeated at most meals, and chores such as setting, clearing, and doing the dishes may be carried out by the same individual over time.

The ritual elements of mealtimes are symbolic and tied to emotions. Ritual communication is symbolic. The use of nicknames, inside jokes, and terms of endearment reinforce individuals' role in the group and hold meaning for those inside the family. The commitment to family rituals is affective and emotional. The emotional bonds created during these repetitive gatherings are played over and over again in memory, contributing to a sense that individuals belong to a group that can be a safe refuge. There is a generational continuity to family mealtimes such that dishes, recipes, and blessings are passed down from one generation to the next. There may also be a repetition of topics of conversation from one meal to the next that serves to reinforce family identity and provides an opportunity to discuss sensitive topics. These aspects of family mealtimes are summarized in Table 5.1.

The routine aspects of family mealtime include instrumental communication, task accomplishment, and repetition of roles over time. Ritual aspects of the meal center on problem solving, affective investment, and the symbolic nature of repetitive interactions. How might these two dimensions be related to the well-being of children and the creation of a family identity? Although the literature is somewhat sparse, we draw from existing research as well as examples drawn from research conducted in our own laboratory. As part of a larger study on family adaptation to a childhood chronic illness, we videotape families during a mealtime. We report on seventy-nine of these families in this chapter. Although the families were recruited to participate in a study focused on family life and pediatric asthma (see Fiese, Wamboldt, & Anbar, 2005), they experience similar

Table 5.1. Routine and Ritual Elements of Mealtimes

	Routine	Ritual
Communication	Instrumental	Symbolic
	Assigns roles	Inside jokes
	Get something done	Problem solving
		Sensitive topics
Commitment	Task oriented	Affective
	Setting, clearing, washing dishes	Recognize feelings
	Focus on food	Focus on group belonging
Continuity	Time limited	Cross-generational
	Role repetition	Symbolic referents (recipes, blessings)
		Future planning

challenges facing most families today: juggling work and home life, keeping track of children's whereabouts, and responding to children's emotional needs. Likewise, these families are typically composed of two to three children with only one with an identifiable illness. Thus, they may be representative of the general population in more ways than they are not. In terms of ethnic background, they are approximately 55 percent Caucasian, 30 percent African American, 4 percent Latino, 2 percent Asian, and 8 percent of mixed ethnic heritages. They are from all socioeconomic backgrounds, predominantly working class, and approximately half of the parents are married. The average age of the target children is eight years. We also collect questionnaire data from the families regarding their practice of other family rituals such as weekends and annual celebrations such as birthdays.

We provide examples taken from transcripts of mealtime conversations that highlight different aspects of family routines and rituals. We then provide correlational evidence from our laboratory examining the relation between mealtime interactions and children's mental health (based on teacher and parent report). To support the relations we find between mealtime behaviors and child mental health in this one study, we also draw from other published reports that demonstrate a connection between the predictable elements of mealtime interactions and children's well-being, as well as literature that supports the link between an emotional investment in family gatherings and children's mental health.

Mealtime Routines

We first examine how communication, commitment, and continuity of the routine elements of mealtime are related to child outcomes. Next, we apply the same lens to the ritual elements of family mealtime.

Communication. Communication during mealtimes can be direct or indirect. Direct means of communication send an unambiguous message such that roles are clearly assigned. Indirect means of communication provide little in the way of behavioral guidance and often leave family members lost as to who is responsible for getting the meal done. We have noted in our observations that when family mealtimes are characterized by direct forms of communication, everyone seems to understand what is expected of them. One family comes to mind as an illustration of this direct form of communication. There are two parents and three children ranging from six to twelve years of age. Before the meal begins, the children move swiftly to set the table, each taking a different role: one places the dishes, one sets the glassware, and one arranges napkins (another returns to refold the napkins, evidently not pleased with the arrangement). Prior to sitting down, the mother calls from the kitchen, "What do you guys want to drink?" Without skipping a beat, one sibling remarks: "You get the milk, I'll get the water." Throughout the meal, there are multiple instances of planning for the future that are clearly communicated. The following serves to illustrate.

MOM (*to Sibling 1*): So for your birthday, we are thinking about going to the Lodge and then come back here for presents and cake and stuff.
SIBLING 1: Strawberry cake.
SIBLING 2: I thought you wanted chocolate.
SIBLING 1: Strawberry shortcake. If I got strawberry shortcake, it could be a little girl like Strawberry Shortcake.
MOM: I think we are going to make our own.
SIBLING 2: I want a Scooby Doo one.
MOM: Okay. We'll think of that when it comes time for your birthday.

In this brief example, the mother engages the family in the preparation for the upcoming birthday party and elicits the siblings' ideas. Everyone gets a turn to talk, and there is an opportunity to consider future events such as the other sibling's birthday. Even in cases where there is the clear exchange of ideas, communication still needs to be directed to keep the family on task. In this same family, the end of the mealtime taping was characterized by the father and two of the siblings getting rather "silly" (according to Mom). The father and daughters were laughing to the point of tears, making it difficult for the mother to clear the table. The mother remarked: "Mommy is cleaning up. I want you to finish. Help me clear the table." While maintaining good humor, communication was directed to keep the family on task so the meal could be completed without further disruption.

We have examined the degree to which this type of direct and clear communication during mealtimes is related to children's mental health. We code mealtime behaviors using a global observational coding scheme, the Mealtime Interaction Coding System (MICS; Dickstein, Hayden, Schiller,

Seifer, & San Antonio, 1994). For the purposes of our discussion, we describe the subscales of Communication, Task Accomplishment, Affect Management, and Interpersonal Involvement (see Table 5.2). We have applied this coding system to seventy-nine mealtimes in seventy-nine families enrolled in the Family Life and Asthma Project. We are primarily interested in the development of internalizing symptoms such as anxiety, as these types of problems are more commonly experienced by children with this chronic condition (McQuaid, 2001). We relied on parent reporting using the Child Behavior Checklist (Achenbach & Rescorla, 2001).

We found that families who used direct forms of communication at the dinner table were less likely to have children with internalizing symptoms (see Figure 5.1). Thus, when communication was direct and there was a clear exchange of information, as illustrated in the conversation about birthday cake, children experience less distress overall.

Other researchers have found that patterns of communication are related to variations in mental health. Adults experiencing depression and other major affective disorders have been noted for higher rates of indirect communication or long periods of silence during interpersonal interaction. In an observational study of family mealtimes where the mother had been diagnosed with a major affective disorder, Dickstein and colleagues found that scores on the MICS distinguished the group of mothers with no psychiatric illness from those who received a diagnosis (Dickstein et al., 1998). The authors do not report on findings directly linking the mealtime interactions with child mental health. However, they do report that problematic parent-child interaction patterns observed with the same parents in a free play setting (Hayden et al., 1998) and indirect forms of communication observed during the mealtime may place the children at increased risk for mental health problems (Seifer et al., 1996). Again, we do not mean to indicate that clear and direct forms of communication cause child well-being, only that it is one element of a healthy mealtime context. Let us now consider how family members exhibit their commitment to the routine aspects of mealtimes.

Commitment. Routine commitment to mealtime expresses itself in how the task is accomplished and how the meal begins and ends. Often there is a focus on the food itself and commitment to ensuring everyone is fed. For some families, food choice deserves little comment, and conversations revolve around events of the day or planning, as in the first example. For other families, there is considerable attention on the food choice of an individual, which can result in a singular commitment to accomplishing the meal in a rigid manner. The following serves to illustrate this rigid pattern:

CHILD: I do not want the turkey.
MOM: You like turkey! I made it special.
GRANDMOTHER: She made it just for you.

Table 5.2. Description of Mealtime Interaction Coding System

Subscale	Description	Poor Functioning	Optimal Functioning
Communication	Information exchange: (1) clear versus masked and (2) direct versus indirect.	Ineffective communication; silence or irrelevant talking. Highly masked and indirect. Incongruence of verbal and nonverbal cues.	Clear and direct. Verbal and nonverbal congruence. Messages acknowledged.
Task accomplishment	Structure of meal. Is a routine followed? Are all members satisfied by the food?	Chaotic. Disruptions are not acknowledged or addressed.	Flexible, smooth transitions, efficient planning, noticeable routine.
Affect management	Appropriateness and relevance of emotional expression. Both production and response are considered.	Difficulty with affective production and response. May include severe restriction of emotion, overproduction, or emotional lability.	Affect enhances family interaction. The range and intensity of emotional expression are appropriate, valued, and encouraged.
Interpersonal involvement	How family members value the activities and concerns of each other. Discussions of thoughts, feelings, and experiences, comfort with proximity, and showing of affection.	Lack of involvement, reflecting only instrumental necessity with little collaboration or symbiotic involvement, lack of privacy, unclear boundaries and few independent decisions made.	Empathic involvement in members' activities and concerns, genuine interest in the activities of others, and respect for autonomy coupled with honest caring.

NEW DIRECTIONS FOR CHILD AND ADOLESCENT DEVELOPMENT • DOI 10.1002/cad

Figure 5.1. Correlations Between Internalizing Symptoms and Family Mealtime Behaviors

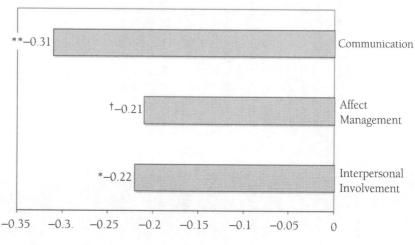

$\dagger p < .10. \ *p < .05. \ **p < .01.$

(*Mom places turkey on child's plate.*)

CHILD: I do not want any! (*Child jumps out of chair and runs from table.*) I said I don't want any!

MOM: But you have to eat something.

CHILD: (*Becomes upset and whines*) But I want the grapes still!

MOM: I will put grapes in a bowl.

CHILD: But I won't even eat that. . . .

DAD: (*interrupts and speaks harshly*) Just sit down and eat your dinner!

GRANDMOTHER: Here, your mommy made this yummy broccoli with cheese sauce.

CHILD: I don't like cheese sauce.

DAD: You like cheese sauce! (*harsh tone*)

CHILD: I would like the cheese sauce if it were made with chocolate milk.

GRANDMOTHER: No, you can't make cheese sauce with chocolate milk. You have to make it with white milk. Chocolate milk is bad for you.

(*Child covers up his eyes and his face. Silence prevails.*)

In this example, there is a committed goal to get the child to eat even in the face of food refusal. Rather than ignoring the child's complaints, the mother and grandmother attempt to cajole him into eating foods that he previously enjoyed. The meal continues, and we observed a pattern of coercion and control similar to that noted by Patterson and colleagues

(Patterson, 1982) whereby the child whines and refuses to participate in a normative task (eating dinner) and ultimately gets his way even in the context of harsh and angry exchanges with the father.

One way to examine whether rigid commitment to conducting the meal is related to poorer child mental health is to identify situations where attention to food choice is a vital part of the meal. Cystic fibrosis is one such condition. Children must adhere to strict dietary guidelines, often causing parental concern about whether the child is consuming enough calories to survive (Speith et al., 2001). In a mealtime observation study of school-age children with cystic fibrosis and healthy matched controls, families with a child with cystic fibrosis were more likely to score in the unhealthy range of accomplishing the mealtime task (Janicke, Mitchell, & Stark, 2005). While the families with a child with cystic fibrosis may be able to get the meal on the table, they may also alter family rules to meet dietary goals through implementing rigid standards for behavior, extending the length of the meal. When mealtime routines are characterized by a rigid focus on consuming particular foods over longer-than-average time periods, there are greater opportunities for squabbles and bickering. Indeed, Stark and colleagues report that it was the average length of mealtime that was related to child behavior problems for children with cystic fibrosis as well as the healthy matched control group (Stark et al., 1997).

In contrast to a rigid commitment to mealtime routines are gatherings characterized by chaos and disorder. In these settings, we observe a considerable amount of movement up and down from the table without clear demarcation of how the meal begins and ends. One way we capture this is through the Task Accomplishment scale of the MICS (see Table 5.2). Using a clinical cut-off score to examine more extreme cases of disorganization where disruptions predominate, we find that family mealtimes marked by chaos have children with elevated internalizing scores on the Child Behavior Checklist ($t(63) = 2.12, p < .04$).

Thus, routine commitment to mealtimes can vary in terms of a rigid focus in accomplishing the task, which can affect the length of mealtime and the course of social interactions. When there is a rigid commitment to having young children eat particular foods, there are greater opportunities for conflicts at the table, which may be associated with problematic child behaviors. In contrast to a rigid focus on food choice are routines marked by a lack of commitment expressed through disorder and few indications of how the meal actually begins and ends. Both extreme variations have implications for children's well-being, with the former resulting in extended periods of bickering and conflict and the latter associated with neglect and disregard. In order to have an effect over time, these routines must be repeated, which brings us to the third element, continuity.

Continuity. Continuity of mealtime routines is probably best illustrated by the frequency with which meals are held. Families who eat together three or four times a week have children who perform better in school, are less likely to engage in risky behavior, and have fewer mental health problems (Compañ, Moreno, Ruiz, & Pascual, 2002; Eisenberg, Olson, Neumark-Sztainer, Story, & Bearinger, 2004). Overall, these survey results suggest that frequency of family meals is associated with more positive child outcomes. What the survey data do not address, however, is the continuity of within-family-level routines.

The optimal way to capture within-family continuity would be through longitudinal studies tracking how topics of conversation and roles are repeated over time. Because we do not have longitudinal evidence from our own mealtime observations at this time, we must draw from other studies as well as speculate on how continuity of roles may be related to child well-being. Folded into mealtime routines are repeated topics of conversation that may serve to regulate some of the outcomes of interest to child development researchers. For example, asking where an adolescent is going after dinner may be a marker of behavior monitoring associated with reduced sexual risk taking (Larson & Almeida, 1999) or checking if a school-age child has homework to do after dinner may be associated with academic success in low-income families (Brody & Flor, 1997). Mealtimes may offer an opportunity to reinforce the importance of roles through repeated topics of conversation. Routines appear to have a developmental course, becoming more regular and organized as children transition from the preschool to elementary school years (Fiese, Hooker, Kotary, & Schwagler, 1993; Fiese et al., 2002) and are associated with academic success in the early elementary school years (Fiese, 2000). Thus, we can speculate that family mealtimes may follow a developmental course similar to other family routines and serve to regulate developmental outcomes over time. A closer examination of mealtime conversations over time may hold clues as to routine continuity in relation to child outcomes.

A central element of routine continuity is the repetition of roles over time. During mealtimes, this may express itself in terms of not only family roles (mother, father, sister, brother) but also roles that individuals take on as part of the family group. For example, we know that parental monitoring is a strong predictor of children's well-being (Furstenberg, Cook, Eccles, Elder, & Sameroff, 1999). When parents keep track of their children's whereabouts and activities, children tend to do better in school.

"Activity monitor" is a role played repeatedly at the dinner table by parents. In Western cultures, conversations at the dinner table are likely to include a focus on the child's daily activities, including what the child did during the day, homework needs, who the child befriends, and what plans need to be made for the future (Blum-Kulka, 1997). These repeated conversations include implicit roles such as student, homework monitor, guardian, and chauffeur. The point to be made here is that routine continuity garners its effect on children's well-being not only through sheer repetition but also through reinforcement of roles and possible influence in arenas such as school performance, peer relationships, and planning for future events. Because of the limited empirical evidence linking repetition of mealtime routine roles to child mental health, we can only speculate on the possible relation. However, the larger literature linking parental monitoring and positive child outcomes suggests that mealtimes may be one setting where such roles are enacted.

Summary. To summarize, direct and clear forms of communication, a flexible rather than rigid or chaotic commitment to carrying out mealtimes, and continuity as evidenced by repetition of roles appear to be associated with children's well-being. The evidence linking direct forms of communication is the strongest and has been demonstrated at multiple sites. As we pointed out in our introductory comments, the study of family mealtimes presents an opportunity to examine social interaction in a group setting. Thus, we find that clear and direct forms of communication observed under naturalistic conditions of family mealtimes show the same positive relation to child mental health as they do when observed in tightly controlled laboratory settings. While this extends our confidence that the effects of clear and direct communication are not limited to the confines of a university laboratory setting, we also learn something about family functioning as a whole.

Family mealtimes are densely packed events. Much has to happen in approximately twenty minutes: food needs to be served and consumed, roles assigned, past events reviewed, and plans made. An efficient way for this densely packed event to happen is through clear and direct forms of communication. An area ripe for future research will be to examine the extent to which the other elements of family routines overlap with communication. Longer mealtimes characterized by more rigid concerns about food consumption were also distinguished by higher levels of cajoling, an indirect form of communication. Thus, rigid commitments to carrying out mealtime routines may not operate independent of indirect forms of communication. The free and open exchange of information may be constrained under conditions of inflexible routines.

Of the three aspects of family mealtime routines, we know the least about continuity and its relation to child mental health. This is an area ripe for future research, as we know very little about within-family continuity and how routines change over time. At its very core, this is a question about developmental transitions and negotiating change. Developmental transition points, such as a child starting middle or high school, are often times when families must consider an alteration in routines. For example, dining at 6:00 P.M. may have made sense when children were in elementary school and homework could easily be done before or after dinner. With teenagers in the home, mealtimes need to be more flexible to accommodate after-school activities and jobs. Future research may address how families provide stability through mealtime routines but also identify how they are altered in form during transition points to accommodate the shifting needs of individuals.

Mealtime Rituals

Whereas routine elements of a mealtime focus on the task at hand, ritual elements center on the emotional and affective realm. In this section, we identify some of the symbolic features of a family mealtime that comprise a ritual. Our discussion of emotions is primarily in reference to sentiments generated during mealtimes. We are not able to catalogue discrete affects such as anger, sadness, or joy in our observations but instead try to capture how family members create a sense of belonging that forms the foundation of family identity.

Communication. Whereas routine elements of mealtime communication focus on the direct exchange of information, ritual elements focus on problem solving, discussion of sensitive topics, and the affective climate. Mealtimes are opportunities for members of the family to work together to solve problems of a sensitive nature, building on personal knowledge of past experiences. The next example illustrates how a relatively mundane conversation evolves into an opportunity to problem-solve and contains elements of respect for the emotions of the five-year-old daughter:

MOTHER: I think the Little Bear [nickname for baby] is not very happy. She looks like she wants to get out of the swing.
FATHER: Yeah, she is not too fond of the swing, not like you were" (*to other child*)
FATHER: What do you think of the cranberry stuff?
CHILD: Good.
FATHER: Oh, yeah? Well we got a lot more if you want more.
CHILD: Well, I didn't actually taste it. I just had a little tiny bit of it.
MOTHER: I tasted the turkey, and it tastes really good.
CHILD: It tastes awesome. It tastes awesome because of the cranberry sauce.
MOTHER: Oh, so you do like the cranberry sauce.
FATHER: (*to child*) Hey, did you straighten out that thing that you were talking to me about during your tubby last night? Did she talk to you about this, Mom? You were saying that people didn't want to play with you.
MOTHER: Why? Who doesn't want to play? I've seen you playing with Shelly and Susan when I come to pick you up.
FATHER: I am still trying to figure out what is going on.
CHILD: Not at the end of the day—at the middle of the day. Like in the afternoon.

MOTHER: Nobody wants to play with you?

FATHER: With after-schoolers?

CHILD: No, not with after-schoolers. Kindergartners.

MOTHER: What do you mean? They don't want to do the same kinds of things that you want to do?

CHILD: Yeah.

MOTHER: Yeah, she was telling me about this before. It's not that they don't want to play, it's that she picks an activity that they are not interested in.

FATHER: Yeah, that was kind of how she was saying it in the tub; it was like they wanted to do different things. But I was trying to explain to her that it wasn't you they didn't want to play with.

MOTHER: Maybe they just wanted to do a different activity.

FATHER: Right. She said she was playing by herself, and that made me kind of sad.

In this example, there are several elements of symbolism and meaning that contribute to the ritual context of family mealtimes. First, we note that the communication includes multiple instances of insider information—complete details of which are accessible only to family members. The baby is affectionately referred to as "Little Bear," a moniker of unknown origin to the outsider but one that is readily understood and not questioned by those at the table. Subtle differences between the older and younger daughter are pointed out (she wants to get out of the swing, not like the older daughter, who liked the swing as an infant), perhaps highlighting temperamental differences between the siblings. The father uses this time as an opportunity to problem-solve around a sensitive issue that was brought up in another routine setting (bath time). The parents identify the multiple meanings behind being rejected by peers and possible solutions to the situation. The father concludes the conversation with a comment reflecting his feelings, perhaps empathizing with his daughter.

Ritual communications build on insider information and make use of knowledge of past experiences that set the frame for family problem solving. In a study of families with young adolescents, Vuchinich (1987) observed bouts of conflicts and their resolution during mealtime. He found that all family members initiated conflict, the bouts were relatively brief, and they served as opportunities to problem-solve. According to the author, the fact that everyone had the right to initiate a conflict bout promoted "open communication and allows everyone to feel as if they have some clout" (p. 599). Because this was a study with young adolescents, we must also consider that the right to initiate a conflict was tied to the deeper meaning of communicating autonomy. In this sense, ritual communications can be embedded in developmental tasks. Similarly, the mealtime conversation with the five year old centered on peer rejection, a developmentally sensitive topic. Ritual communication at mealtimes associated with poorer outcomes would be characterized by ineffective problem solving and an atmosphere that discourages the discussion of sensitive topics.

We do not have direct evidence linking ritual communication at mealtimes with child mental health. However, we have found that symbolic elements of family rituals overall are related to more optimal outcomes. We have developed a questionnaire that reflects the affective and symbolic nature of family rituals. Responding to questions about dinnertime, weekends, special celebrations (birthdays), and vacations, family members who report these events hold special meaning and have symbolic significance are considered highly ritualized (Fiese & Kline, 1993). Previous research has found that when parents report that their family rituals overall hold more symbolic meaning, then there is a greater likelihood that their children will experience less emotional distress (Fiese, 1992; Fiese & Kline, 1993). In the observations of the seventy-nine families described here, parents who ascribed more symbolic meaning to their family rituals were observed using more direct forms of communication during the mealtime ($r = .29$, $p < .01$). The symbolic and ritualized aspects of communication during mealtime may be best supported under the context of routine communications that are open and direct. It is likely that the meaning behind ritualized communications will have greater force (and be understood) when they are relayed in a context that supports the free and open exchange of ideas. Thus, as we noted earlier, the routine element of direct communication may overlap with other routine and ritual aspects of mealtimes. Direct communication may facilitate the creation of deeper symbolic meanings; indirect or inefficient forms of communication may disrupt the process and result in incoherent and disjointed representations. Whereas we have little direct evidence linking ritual communication at mealtimes with child mental health outcomes, the evidence for ritual commitment is more direct.

Commitment. The ritual elements of commitment to mealtime are best illustrated through the emotional investments made in responding to others and maintaining a sense of group cohesiveness. In the conversation noted between the parents and their five-year-old daughter, the parents expressed concern about how their daughter felt when other children wanted to play a different activity. We have noted that mealtimes are often settings where children and parents not only talk about sensitive topics but also reflect on how they feel. This provides an opportunity for validation of emotions and assurance that others share concern about your feelings. We have been able to capture the ritual elements of commitment in mealtimes through the coding of Affect Management and Interpersonal Involvement on the MICS (see Table 5.2). When mealtime interactions are characterized by a genuine concern about others' activities and emotions are well regulated, then children are less likely to experience internalizing symptoms (see

Figure 5.1). These are not necessarily long and drawn-out conversations that involve an in-depth analysis of individual feelings and motives. Rather, they are folded seamlessly into the stream of conversation, somewhere between the cranberry sauce and a second helping of turkey.

As we found with ritual communication, there is a certain degree of overlap between what we observe as ritual commitment during the mealtime and parents' overall commitment to family rituals. In this group of seventy-nine families, the two aspects of ritual commitment observed during mealtimes were directly related to parent report of how much meaning they ascribed to their family rituals (affect management $r = .33$, $p < .002$; interpersonal involvement $r = .36$, $p < .001$). These findings suggest that when families express concern about other's feelings and an interest in other's activities during mealtimes, they also value family gatherings such as weekend activities and birthday celebrations as opportunities for special times together. In previous reports, we have found that this deep affective commitment to family rituals provides a sense of belonging and trust associated with adolescent and relational well-being (Fiese, 1992; Fiese et al., 1993).

When we considered the routine elements of commitment, we noted that rigid patterns focused on food choice and extended mealtimes characterized by increased opportunities for bickering were more likely to be associated with poor child mental health. In the case of ritual commitment, we note that respect for others' feelings and genuine concern about others' activities are associated with more positive outcomes. Thus, when we consider the deeper meanings behind commitment, what may appear on the surface as a routine disagreement over what an individual chooses to eat may evolve into personal feelings of disregard and rejection. In order for these feelings to take hold, the experiences must be repeated over time, which brings us to ritual continuity.

Continuity. Ritual continuity of mealtimes can be seen in at least two ways. First is continuity in group cohesion. In order for the group to be maintained over time, planning must take place. This is essentially a symbolic activity that holds meaning for the family, as planning also involves an element that preserves memories of gatherings over time. The symbolic continuity resides in the mutual understanding of those gathered together that the group will survive. Second is ritual continuity between two or more generations. Ritual practices are often passed down from one generation to the next. The symbolism behind these practices offers continuity of meaning across generations, affecting beliefs about family relationships. Let us first consider how planning contributes to mealtime ritual continuity.

In order to endure as a group, someone needs to plan. Planning is an important part of ritual continuity. In several factor analytical studies, we have found that deliberate planning for events such as dinnertime and weekends is more closely aligned with the affective and symbolic aspects of rituals than it is with the routine elements (Fiese, 1992; Fiese et al., 1993;

Fiese & Kline, 1993; Markson & Fiese, 2000). There are at least two reasons for this finding. First, planning is at its very core a representational skill (Haith, 1997). In order to plan for the future, it has to be conceptualized. Although we typically think about meal planning as constructing a menu or a grocery list, the ritual elements of planning include constructing images, or representations, of relationships that define these gatherings. These images may be more vivid when considering planning for elaborate events such as a Thanksgiving meal. Considering when everyone is going to arrive or where everyone is going to sit may be cause for careful planning, particularly if there has been a change in the family as through marriage, divorce, or remarriage. However, the same symbolic process may be in force during more routine mealtimes throughout the course of the week. Planning for the future may stabilize the group by solving problems before they escalate, keeping everyone informed about others' activities, and placing value on the goals and needs of individuals. In our study of these seventy-nine families, we ask whether dinnertimes in general are planned ahead or tend to be on the spur of the moment. We have found that when families report more deliberate planning around mealtimes, they are also less likely to report internalizing problems in their children ($r = -.31, p < .01$).

The second way that ritual continuity expresses itself in mealtimes is the influence of the family of origin on current family practices. Many of the subtleties observed during mealtime are rooted in practices that parents experienced in their own childhoods. In interviews of families about their family-of-origin experiences, we have found that mealtimes are often sources of vivid memories (Fiese, in press). Family members recount that they may have changed times at which they eat, but they aim to preserve family meals as a set-aside time to be together. In these anecdotal accounts, parents remark that they use some of the same serving dishes or say the same blessings that they did as children. Just as deliberate planning included a representational aspect linked to family relationships, there are also representational elements to intergenerational continuity of rituals. In a previous report, we described a study of fifty families where we asked parents to tell a story to their child about a dinnertime when the parent was growing up. We examined the degree to which family-of-origin relationships at the mealtime were depicted as trustworthy and warm. Furthermore, we compared these representations of family-of-origin relationships with patterns of interaction observed at the dinner table with the parents and their own children (Fiese & Marjinsky, 1999). We found a generational continuity between the themes in the stories about mealtime in the parents' generation and the interaction patterns observed between parents and children. Parents who recounted their family-of-origin mealtimes as warm, supportive, and opportunities to gather together as a group were more likely to express positive affect at the dinner table with their own children. Their children were also less likely to evidence problematic behaviors.

Whereas the continuity of mealtime routines was most clearly seen in the repetition of roles, the continuity of mealtime rituals is embedded in symbolism. We note that deliberate planning links events in time from one day to the next and, in some cases, may include links from one generation to the next. This is a representational act whereby family members construct images of what happens during collective mealtime gatherings. These representations, or beliefs about family relationships, may serve to guide behavior in routine settings (Fiese & Sameroff, 1999). By examining how symbolic representations of relationships are embedded in family mealtime interactions repeated over time, we get a glimpse at how the continuity of rituals may contribute to child mental health. This is clearly an area that is in its empirical infancy and warrants further attention.

Mealtime Rituals and Family Identity

Throughout this chapter, we have referred to mealtime as a context in which family identity is formed. Rituals in general may contribute to family identity within the dimension of group support (Fiese, in press). When family members are generally supportive of each other, an identity is formed that values group membership and is built around themes of inclusion. Many of the examples we have provided here fit into that realm. In other cases, alienation predominates, and family identity is built around themes of exclusion. We can consider family identity as an integration of the ritual elements of communication, commitment, and continuity. The last example drawn from our mealtime observations serves to illustrate a case of family identity that revolves around alienation. This case incorporates several elements under discussion, including how the meal begins, affective investment, and representation of relationships. This is a mealtime conversation between a nine-year-old child and a single parent:

MOTHER: You can start eating.
CHILD: I got to say grace.
MOTHER: I don't go through all that. I just eat. So you think that's the proper way to do it? To say grace?
CHILD: Aren't you going to say grace?
MOTHER: You just say what you want to say. I'm just going to say eat the food.
CHILD: Bless this food and those people who don't have anything to eat.

The meal continues with long gaps in the conversation, and the television is on in the background. At one point, the child considers whom to approach for a school fund drive. The mother comments that no one will buy anything because "By the things people do, you know who wants to be bothered and who don't. I don't like to be bothered. It's people who are the problem." The child tries to engage the mother in the conversation and considers selling to a relative who recently gave the child ten dollars. The child reveals sharing the money with a cousin. This upsets the mother, who comments: "What reason did you have to share?" At this point, the child leaves the table.

The identity conveyed throughout this mealtime conversation is one of exclusion and lack of trust in others. Relationships are seen as a bother rather than a source of reward, and planning revolves around how to avoid others rather than relying on others as sources of support. According to her teacher's report, this child scored in the clinical range of internalizing problems and showed symptoms consistent with an anxiety disorder. We have found in previous studies that when there is little meaning ascribed to family rituals, children are at heightened risk for developing anxiety-related symptoms (Markson & Fiese, 2000). We speculate that when rituals are marked by patterns of exclusion and used for opportunities to degrade rather than support, group membership is compromised, and family identity is characterized by alienation. Indeed, one would question why anyone would want to belong to such a group.

Conclusion

We conclude with a discussion of the strongest evidence linking mealtime routines and rituals to child mental health, how researchers may consider the overlapping dimensions of communication, commitment, and continuity in future research, and a message for busy families.

We think this research points to important aspects of family mealtimes for the well-being of children. The most consistent evidence for explaining these benefits is found in research linking communication patterns with child outcomes. Throughout our observations of family mealtimes and our reading of the, albeit limited, literature, it strikes us that clear and direct communication at the dinner table is an essential ingredient for a healthy family meal. As a routine, the free exchange of information may make it easier to get the task done, which may reduce some of the stresses associated with trying to feed a hungry group.

Beyond task accomplishment is the role that clear and direct communication plays in supporting positive emotional exchanges within the family. This is important for several reasons. First, positive emotional support is associated with better mental health for all family members. Validating feelings and knowing that the family provides a safe place to express troubling thoughts can most optimally occur when these thoughts are relayed in a clear manner. Second, when emotions can be expressed in a safe place, there are added opportunities for problem solving. Whether it is being rejected by peers in kindergarten or a difficult conversation with a coworker, being able to problem-solve with other family members may provide multiple solutions to a difficult situation and also send the implicit message that your voice will be heard. A third reason that clear and direct communication at the dinner table is essential to family health is linked to our emphasis on the symbolic nature of family rituals. Family system researchers and therapists have long been aware that family communications often convey symbolic meanings that only those inside the family can understand. We used for our example the case of nicknames because it is something, as outsiders, we can identify. However, family members typically have their own ways of communicating the deeper meanings of what it means to be a member of the family. If these deeper meanings are communicated in a direct and clear manner, we suspect that the symbolic representations that are formed are more coherent, and family relationships will be seen as trustworthy. We do not have direct evidence from our mealtime studies to support this speculation. However, previous research has supported the link between coherent accounts of family events and trustworthiness of relationships (Fiese & Sameroff, 1999).

It is not only clear and direct communication that is related to the children's well-being. We also note that when there is a rigid commitment to conducting the meal in a prescribed manner, there are increased opportunities for bickering and squabbling. In contrast to rigid commitments, there is also some indication that chaotic mealtimes are associated with less optimal child outcomes. Clear and direct communication is unlikely to be supported in either rigidly organized or chaotic environments. We noted that rigid attention to food choice was associated with cajoling, a form of indirect communication. Other researchers have noted that when there are elevated levels of chaos in the household, there is a reduced ability to understand and respond to social cues (Dumas et al., 2005). We conclude that communication and commitment during mealtimes operate synergistically with the overall commitment to mealtime routines, lending itself to either the clear and direct exchange of information or being disrupted to the extent that communication is compromised. It is under these compromised conditions that children's well-being is also compromised.

In our introductory comments, we identified two reasons that psychologists might be interested in the study of family mealtimes. We proposed that family mealtime behavior may be consistent with other patterns of social interaction known to be associated with good or poor childhood outcomes. There is increasing evidence to suggest that chaos in the environment is related to poor socioemotional functioning (Evans, Gonnella, Marcynyszyn, Gentile, & Salpekar, 2005). Thus, observations made in family homes during twenty-minute mealtimes are consistent with observations made in larger social ecologies. We also proposed that mealtimes form part of the symbolic foundation of family life. Whereas routine commitment may indicate standards for behavior that are commensurate with what we know about other social interaction patterns that support or disrupt mental health, it is the synergistic exchange between routine and ritual commitment that offers a more complete story about how emotions contribute to a family's sense of identity. When a family invests its concern in others, even in something as simple as planning for a birthday party, an identity is formed that centers on belongingness rather than exclusion. When the meaning behind ritual commitment includes opportunities to deride others, identity is aligned with alienation. Thus, when families communicate their concern, they also communicate their commitment.

We have presented the routine and ritual elements of mealtimes as distinct from each other. We are able to identify aspects of mealtime conversations and interactions that align with communication, commitment, and continuity of routines and rituals. However, just as a meal is composed of different courses that sometimes overlap, these elements too cross boundaries. This is not to say the distinctions are not useful, but it does reinforce the notion that mealtimes are multifaceted enterprises. What starts out as a routine inquiry about what happened in school can evolve into the recognition of an upsetting situation peppered with the use of a nickname meant to provide comfort and assurance that problems can be solved in the confines of this accepting group. Typically this type of routine exchange may last but a few moments. Its ritual roots, however, may extend across several generations.

It is this overlap among dimensions that may be fruitful for future research. How is commitment communicated? How are decisions made about how much time to spend in collective mealtimes that lead to continuity over time? There appear to be at least three areas that may bear fruit in this regard. First is a focus on developmental transitions. With each new phase of family life, there is often a redefining of roles and expansion or contraction of close relationships. Mealtimes may be one setting where transitions are keenly seen. For example, the routine commitment to mealtime may need to be altered when adolescents hold jobs or are engaged in after-school activities. Ritual communications may also change for families with adolescents as the meaning behind increasing levels of autonomy and independence is reinforced and negotiated.

Second, how do families go about the process of making decisions about how they commit to family routines and rituals? There appears to be a curvilinear feature to commitment. Too much commitment can result in a rigid pattern, whereas too lax a commitment results in chaos. We proposed that deliberate planning may be one avenue of influence. Future research may identify others.

Third, how does the meaning of family mealtimes shift with time? This is a relatively unexplored topic. Yet we know that how family members make sense of their family-of-origin mealtimes is associated with how they conduct themselves at the dinner table (Fiese & Marjinsky, 1999). Are there points in the family life cycle where the meaning of family meals shifts so that what was once an eagerly anticipated event becomes a burden? Do life events, such as illness or divorce, result in a redefinition of what family mealtimes mean to individuals? These are a few of the questions that may be addressed in future research.

What can the busy family with a full plate take away from this work? Family mealtimes are densely packed affairs. How family members communicate affects not only how well the job gets done but also reflects the roles that members play and provides opportunities to problem-solve around sensitive topics. A commitment to family mealtimes that is neither rigidly focused on food choice nor chaotic in its beginning and ending will likely present fewer opportunities for conflict. Being emotionally involved and genuinely committed to learning about the daily activities of others will likely result in feelings of belonging and group cohesiveness. Establishing continuity in the dinnertime routine through planning for the future evokes not only a grocery list but memories of relationships and opportunities to create memories that extend across two or more generations. Does this need to be a lengthy and elaborate event that happens like clockwork seven nights a week? Probably not. It is unlikely—given the multiple demands on family members' time—that everyone collectively is at home at the same time every evening. However, planning ahead a few nights a week may be sufficient to preserve this important ritual. Mealtime behavior and the symbolic significance of family rituals are part and parcel of the evolving nature of family identity and the process of integrating the individual into this very special group.

References

Achenbach, T. M., & Rescorla, L. A. (2001). *Manual for the ASEBA school-age forms and profiles*. Burlington: University of Vermont, Research Center for Children, Youth and Families.

Blum-Kulka, S. (1997). *Dinner talk: Cultural patterns of socialization in family discourse*. Mahwah, NJ: Erlbaum.

Brody, G. H., & Flor, D. L. (1997). Maternal psychological functioning, family processes, and child adjustment in rural, single-parent, African American families. *Developmental Psychology, 33*, 1000–1011.

Compañ, E., Moreno, J., Ruiz, M. T., & Pascual, E. (2002). Doing things together: Adolescent health and family rituals. *Journal of Epidemiology and Community Health, 56*, 89–94.

Dickstein, S., Hayden, L. C., Schiller, M., Seifer, R., & San Antonio, W. (1994). Providence Family Study mealtime family interaction coding system. Adapted from the McMaster Clinical Rating Scale. East Providence, RI: E. P. Bradley Hospital.

Dickstein, S., Seifer, R., Hayden, L. C., Schiller, M., Sameroff, A. J., Keitner, G. I., Miller, I., Rasmussen, S., Matzko, M., & Magee, K. D. (1998). Levels of family assessment: II. Impact of maternal psychopathology on family functioning. *Journal of Family Psychology, 12*(1),23–40.

Dickstein, S., St. Andre, M., Sameroff, A. J., Seifer, R., & Schiller, M. (1999). Maternal depression, family functioning, and child outcomes: A narrative assessment. In B. H. Fiese, A. J. Sameroff, H. D. Grotevant, F. S. Wamboldt, S. Dickstein, & D. L. Fravel (Eds.), *The stories that families tell: Narrative coherence, narrative interaction, and* relationship beliefs. *Monographs of the Society for Research in Child Development, 64*(2, Serial No. 257, pp. 84–104). Malden, MA: Blackwell.

Dumas, J. E., Nissley, J., Nordstrom, A., Smith, E. P., Prinz, R. J., & Levine, D. W. (2005). Home chaos: Sociodemographic, parenting, interactional, and child correlates. *Journal of Clinical Child and Adolescent Psychology, 34,* 93–104.

Eisenberg, M. E., Olson, R. E., Neumark-Sztainer, D., Story, M., & Bearinger, L. H. (2004). Correlations between family meals and psychosocial well-being among adolescents. *Archives of Pediatric and Adolescent Medicine, 158,* 792–796.

Evans, G. W., Gonnella, C., Marcynyszyn, L. A., Gentile, L., & Salpekar, N. (2005). The role of chaos in poverty and children's socioemotional adjustment. *Psychological Science, 16,* 560–565.

Fiese, B. H. (1992). Dimensions of family rituals across two generations: Relation to adolescent identity. *Family Process, 31,* 151–162.

Fiese, B. H. (2000). Family matters: A systems view of family effects on children's cognitive health. In R. J. Sternberg & E. L. Grigorenko (Eds.), *Environmental effects on cognitive abilities* (pp. 39–57). Mahwah, NJ: Erlbaum.

Fiese, B. H. (in press). *Family routines and rituals: Promising prospects for the 21st century.* New Haven, CT: Yale University Press.

Fiese, B. H., Hooker, K. A., Kotary, L., & Schwagler, J. (1993). Family rituals in the early stages of parenthood. *Journal of Marriage and the Family, 57,* 633–642.

Fiese, B. H., & Kline, C. A. (1993). Development of the Family Ritual Questionnaire: Initial reliability and validation studies. *Journal of Family Psychology, 6,* 1–10.

Fiese, B. H., & Marjinsky, K.A.T. (1999). Dinnertime stories: Connecting relationship beliefs and child behavior. In B. H. Fiese, A. J. Sameroff, H. D. Grotevant, F. S. Wamboldt, S. Dickstein, & D. Fravel (Eds.), *The stories that families tell: Narrative coherence, narrative interaction, and relationship beliefs, Monographs of the Society for Research in Child Development, 64*(2, Serial No. 257, pp. 52–68). Malden, MA: Blackwell.

Fiese, B. H., & Sameroff, A. J. (1999). The family narrative consortium: A multidimensional approach to narratives. In B. H. Fiese, A. J. Sameroff, H. D. Grotevant, F. S. Wamboldt, S. Dickstein, & D. L. Fravel (Eds.), *The stories that families tell: Narrative coherence, narrative interaction, and relationship beliefs. Monographs of the Society for Research in Child Development, 64*(2, Serial No. 257, pp. 1–36). Malden, MA: Blackwell.

Fiese, B. H., Tomcho, T., Douglas, M., Josephs, K., Poltrock, S., & Baker, T. (2002). Fifty years of research on naturally occurring rituals: Cause for celebration? *Journal of Family Psychology, 16,* 381–390.

Fiese, B. H., Wamboldt, F. S., & Anbar, R. D. (2005). Family asthma management routines: Connections to medical adherence and quality of life. *Journal of Pediatrics, 146,* 171–176.

Furstenberg, F. F., Cook, T. D., Eccles, J., Elder, G. H., & Sameroff, A. J. (1999). *Managing to make it: Urban families and adolescent success.* Chicago: University of Chicago Press.

Haith, M. M. (1997). The development of future thinking as essential for the emergence of skill in planning. In S. L. Friedman & E. K. Scholnick (Eds.), *The developmental psychology of planning: Why, how, and when do we plan?* (pp. 25–42). Mahwah, NJ: Erlbaum.

Hayden, L. C., Schiller, M., Dickstein, S., Seifer, R., Sameroff, A. J., Miller, I., Keitner, G., & Rasmussen, S. (1998). Levels of family assessment I: Family, marital, and parent-child interaction. *Journal of Family Psychology, 12,* 7–22.

Janicke, D. M., Mitchell, M. J., & Stark, L. J. (2005). Family functioning in school-age children with cystic fibrosis: An observational assessment of family interactions in the mealtime environment. *Journal of Pediatric Psychology, 30,* 179–186.

Larson, R. W., & Almeida, D. M. (1999). Emotional transmission in the daily lives of families: A new paradigm for studying family process. *Journal of Marriage and the Family, 61,* 5–20.

Markson, S., & Fiese, B. H. (2000). Family rituals as a protective factor for children with asthma. *Journal of Pediatric Psychology, 25*(7), 471–479.

McQuaid, E. L. (2001). Behavioral adjustment in children with asthma: A meta-analysis. *Journal of Developmental and Behavioral Pediatrics, 22,* 430–439.

Patterson, G. R. (1982). *Coercive family process.* Eugene, OR: Castalia.

Seifer, R., Sameroff, A. J., Dickstein, S., Keitner, G., Miller, I., Rasmussen, S., & Hayden, L. C. (1996). Parental psychopathology, multiple contextual risks, and one-year outcomes in children. *Journal of Clinical Child Psychology, 25,* 423–435.

Speith, L. E., Stark, L. J., Mitchell, M. J., Schiller, M., Cohen, L. L., Mulvihill, M., & Hovell, M. F. (2001). Observational assessment of family functioning at mealtime in preschool children with cystic fibrosis. *Journal of Family Psychology, 26,* 215–224.

Stark, L. J., Mulvihill, M. M., Jelalian, E., Bowen, A., Powers, S. W., Tao, S., Cleveling, S., Passero, M. A., Harwood, I., Light, M., Lapey, A., & Hovell, M. F. (1997). Descriptive analysis of eating behavior in school-age children with cystic fibrosis and healthy control children. *Pediatrics, 99,* 665–671.

Vuchinich, S. (1987). Starting and stopping spontaneous family conflicts. *Journal of Marriage and the Family, 49,* 591–601.

Barbara H. Fiese is professor and chair of psychology at Syracuse University.

Kimberly P. Foley is a former project coordinator of the Family Life and Asthma Project at Syracuse University and is currently a graduate student in child-clinical psychology at West Virginia University.

Mary Spagnola is a doctoral candidate in clinical psychology at Syracuse University and a National Head Start Dissertation Scholar.

6

Adolescents are at risk for poor dietary intake and unhealthy weight control behaviors. Family meals appear to play an important role in helping adolescents make healthier food choices and avoid engaging in unhealthy weight control and binge eating behaviors.

Eating Among Teens: Do Family Mealtimes Make a Difference for Adolescents' Nutrition?

Dianne Neumark-Sztainer

Adolescence is a period of rapid growth and development. Energy and nutrient needs in adolescence are higher than during any other period of the life span (Story, Holt, & Sofka, 2000). It is somewhat ironic that during this period of high dietary needs, various forces interact to make it challenging for adolescents to make healthy food choices. A major task of adolescence is to establish one's own identity, which involves a process of separation from one's parents. Adolescents become more autonomous and spend more time away from home and family than they did when they were younger. Thus, although their parents continue to be a major influence on their eating patterns, peers and broader social influences tend to become stronger. Adolescents are the target of advertisements for fast food restaurants, soft drinks, and foods that tend to be high in calories and low in nutrients. As a result, many adolescents are not meeting recommendations for dietary intake, and a high percentage of youth are overweight. According to the U.S. Department of Agriculture (USDA) Health Index Rating, 94 percent of children between ages thirteen and eighteen years show poor-quality diets or diets in need of improvement (Lino, Gerrior, Basiotis, & Anand, 1998). Our research team has found that 70 percent of adolescent girls and 57 percent of adolescent boys eat less than the recommended amount of calcium (1300 milligrams per day or more); 68 percent of girls and 71 percent of boys eat fewer than five servings of fruits and vegetables a day; 48 percent of girls

NEW DIRECTIONS FOR CHILD AND ADOLESCENT DEVELOPMENT, no. 111, Spring 2006 © Wiley Periodicals, Inc.
Published online in Wiley InterScience (www.interscience.wiley.com) • DOI: 10.1002/cad.156

and 55 percent of boys eat too much fat (more than 30 percent of their calories from fat); and 33 percent of girls and 31 percent of boys are overweight or at risk for becoming overweight (Neumark-Sztainer, Story, Hannan, & Croll, 2002).

Although adolescents appear not to be overly concerned about their nutrition and health, many teens are concerned about their weight. Adolescents, particularly adolescent girls, face intense pressures to be thin. Pressures to be thin come from within the family and from social influences beyond the family. Although it is desirable for youth to engage in behaviors aimed at healthy weight management, research shows that many adolescents are engaging in unhealthy weight control behaviors (Story, French, Resnick, & Blum, 1995; Neumark-Sztainer & Hannan, 2000; Serdula et al., 1993). Ironically, overly restrictive dieting practices may lead to binge eating behaviors, which may have the unintended result of weight gain. In a large study of adolescents, 57 percent of adolescent girls and 33 percent of adolescent boys reported the use of one or more of the following behaviors aimed at weight control over the past year: skipping meals, eating very little food, using a food substitute, fasting, or smoking more cigarettes (Neumark-Sztainer, Story, Hannan, Perry, and Irving, 2002). Extreme weight control behaviors, including vomiting or use of laxatives, diet pills, or diuretics, were reported by 12 percent of the girls and 5 percent of the boys. Binge eating was reported by 17 percent of the adolescent girls and 8 percent of the adolescent boys.

Given these concerns with teens' nutrition and dieting, it is important to examine the role that families do and can play in influencing adolescents' eating patterns, weight concerns, and dieting behaviors. What is the role of family meals? To what extent are adolescents eating with their families? Do adolescents who eat more frequently with their families have higher-quality diets? What aspects of family meals, aside from their frequency, are associated with the use of disordered eating behaviors, such as unhealthy weight control and binge eating behaviors in teens?

Our research team has examined family meals in the homes of adolescents and the associations between family meal patterns and eating patterns in adolescents using qualitative and quantitative research methodologies. The aim of this chapter is to summarize some of the key findings from our research and other large, population-based studies that have examined associations between family mealtime patterns and eating among teens.

Family Meals in the Homes of Teens: What Do They Look Like, and How Often Do They Occur?

Very few studies have examined the relationship between family mealtimes and the quality of teens' diets. Our research team set out to learn what family mealtimes looked like among teens from different backgrounds and how the characteristics and frequency of these mealtimes related to adolescents' intake of nutrients. Project EAT (Eating Among Teens) was designed to examine socioenvironmental, personal, and behavioral factors associated with dietary intake and weight issues in a diverse population of adolescents. The study included (1) twenty-one focus groups with 141 middle school and high school adolescents; (2) surveys and anthropometric (for example, growth) assessments of 4,746 adolescents in the 1998–1999 school year; and (3) telephone interviews with a sample of 902 parents of the participants who completed surveys. In addition, in 2004, we completed the collection of five-year follow-up data on 2,516 of the original study participants, which we have just begun to analyze (and are not discussed in this chapter).

The sample for Project EAT was drawn from thirty-one public schools in urban Minnesota that served ethnically and socioeconomically diverse communities. The mean age of the 4,746 participants was 14.9 years (range 11 to 18 years); a third were in middle school, and two-thirds were in high school. The racial/ethnic backgrounds of the participants were as follows: 48 percent white, 19 percent African American, 19 percent Asian American, 6 percent Hispanic, 4 percent Native American, and 4 percent mixed/other.

The first stage of the project included focus group discussions with adolescents to explore factors that they perceived as influencing their eating patterns and food choices (Neumark-Sztainer, Story, Perry, & Casey, 1999; Neumark-Sztainer, Story, Ackard, Moe, & Perry, 2000). A number of questions focused on learning more about meal patterns in families with adolescents. Findings indicated great diversity in the frequency of family meals in the homes of adolescents. Some of the teens talked about having family meals on a regular basis in their homes. Others said that family meals occurred very rarely in their homes, primarily due to busy schedules of teens and their parents. Adolescents whose parents lived in separate homes often reported different mealtime routines in each home. For example, one teen said that at his mother's home, he eats family meals on a daily basis, while at his father's home, family meals do not usually happen. Family meals also looked very different in different homes. Some adolescents talked about eating around the kitchen table with the whole family present, others described eating in the living room with their family while watching television, and still others described taking food up to their bedrooms and eating alone in front of the television.

This variability in family eating patterns was found in the survey data of Project EAT as well (Neumark-Sztainer, Hannan, Story, Croll, & Perry, 2003). Frequency of family meals was assessed with the survey question, "During the past seven days, how many times did all, or most, of your family living in your house eat a meal together?" Response categories were "never," "1–2 times," "3–4 times," "5–6 times," "7 times," and "more than 7 times." The adolescents' responses to this question (with several categories combined) were as follows: never (girls: 12 percent; boys: 16 percent), one to two times (19 percent; 20 percent), three to six times (43 percent; 37 percent), and seven or more times (26 percent; 27 percent). Thus, approximately one-third of the teens reported eating two or fewer family meals in the past week, and approximately one-fourth reported eating family meals on a daily basis (seven or more times in the past week).

We also found differences in family meal frequency by sociodemographic characteristics (see Figure 6.1) (Neumark-Sztainer, Hannan, et al. 2003). Family meals were found to be more frequent among youth from higher socioeconomic backgrounds. Asian American teens reported eating more family meals per week than did their white, African American, Hispanic, or Native American counterparts. Although gender differences were small, girls reported eating somewhat fewer family meals per week than boys did. Large differences were found by age, with middle school students reporting a greater number of family meals per week than their older high school peers. Finally, the vast majority (90 percent) of mothers in the study were employed, and teens whose mothers worked full time reported eating fewer family meals per week than did teens whose mothers worked fewer hours or were not employed. In sum, family meals were more frequent among teens who were from higher socioeconomic backgrounds, Asian American, male, younger, and had mothers who worked fewer hours.

These findings demonstrate that there is diversity in family meal patterns in the homes of adolescents. In some homes, families gather around the table to eat together, while in other homes, adolescents eat by themselves in front of the television. In some homes, family meals are the norm, while in other homes, family meals are a rarity. Many families lie in between these two extremes. From focus group discussions, we learned that busy schedules of teens and their parents have a large influence on the frequency of family meals. From survey data, we found that family meal frequency differed by family characteristics, like ethnicity and parents' work schedules, and teen characteristics, particularly age. These findings indicate that researchers and practitioners discussing family meals with teens and parents should not make assumptions about family meal patterns. Learning how frequently family meals occur, when they occur, and about factors that influence family meal patterns are important first steps in understanding how mealtimes may influence eating among teens.

Family Meals and Dietary Intake in Adolescents

Since nutrient needs are so high during adolescence and many teens are not eating in accordance with dietary recommendations, it is important to understand how these differences in family meal patterns might influence the quality of dietary intake among adolescents. Three large population-based studies have examined associations between family meal patterns and

Figure 6.1. Rate of Family Mealtimes per Week by Maternal Employment, Teen's Age, Gender, Ethnicity, and Socioeconomic Status

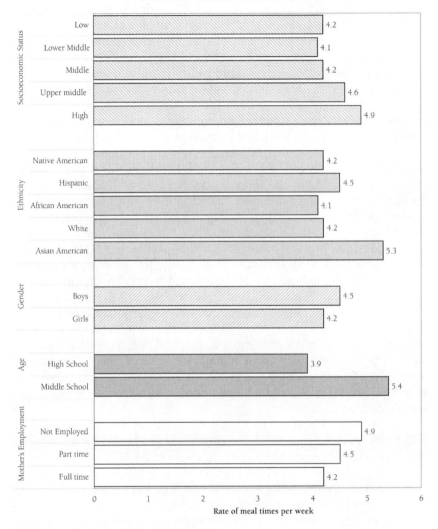

All differences are statistically significant: $p < .001$.

Source: This figure is based on data from Neumark-Sztainer, Hannan, et al. (2003).

adolescents' food consumption: Project EAT, the Growing Up Today Study, and the Add Health Study.

In Project EAT, we examined the associations between frequency of family meals and dietary intake among adolescents (Neumark-Sztainer, Hannan, et al., 2003). Frequency of family meals was assessed using the same question described above. Dietary intake was assessed with the 149-item Youth and Adolescent Food Frequency Questionnaire (YAQ) (Rockett et al., 1997; Rockett, Wolf, & Colditz, 1995). Servings of fruits, vegetables, grains, calcium-rich foods, snack foods, and soft drinks were examined. In addition, we assessed adolescents' intake of a number of key nutrients.

The analyses revealed a clear relationship between family mealtimes and the quality of teens' diets. Frequency of family meals in the past week was found to be positively and significantly associated with adolescents' intake of fruits, vegetables, grains, and calcium-rich foods. As can be seen in Figure 6.2, fruit and vegetable intake steadily increased with each increase in family meal frequency. Adolescents reporting seven or more family meals in the past week had an average of one serving more of fruits and vegetables each day than adolescents reporting no family meals in the past week. Frequency of family meals in the past week was negatively associated with soft drink intake and was not associated with snack frequency. Strong, positive associations were also found between family meal frequency and intakes of energy; percentage of calories from protein; calcium; iron; vitamins A, C, E, B6, folate; and fiber. For example, mean daily calcium intake (in milligrams) was as follows: no family meals (M = 870); one to two meals (M = 955); three to six meals (1,036); seven or more meals (M = 1,096). All of these trends were found to remain significant after adjusting for sociodemographic characteristics, except the association for vitamin E. Significant associations were not found between frequency of family meals and the percentage of total calories from total fats and saturated fats, and only small differences were found in carbohydrate intake as a percentage of total calories. In summary, the Project EAT data indicate that middle school and high school adolescents who ate more meals with their families consumed more healthy foods and were less likely to consume soft drinks.

The Growing Up Today Study (GUTS), conducted by Gillman and his colleagues (2000), examined associations between family meal frequency and quality of dietary intake in older children and adolescents (ages nine to fourteen years). The study population included 16,202 sons and daughters of participants in the ongoing Nurses' Health Study II, a study of female registered nurses in the United States. The majority (93 percent) of the respondents were white. Thus, the GUTS study population tended to be younger and more homogeneous in terms of ethnicity and socioeconomic status than the Project EAT study population, but was drawn from a broader geographical area. Family meal frequency was assessed with a question that focused on evening meals: "How often do you sit down with other members of your family to eat dinner or supper?" Dietary intake was assessed with the same food frequency questionnaire used in Project EAT. Additional questions were asked about frequency of consuming ready-made dinners and other eating and activity behaviors.

Figure 6.2. Rate of Fruit and Vegetable Consumption by Family Meals per Week

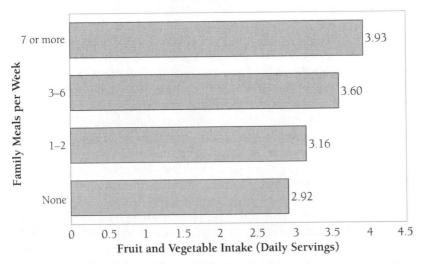

Source: This figure is based on data from Neumark-Sztainer, Hannan, et al. (2003).

As in Project EAT, there was diversity in the frequency of family meals. The youth reported eating dinner with their family at the following rates: never or some days (17 percent), most days (40 percent), and every day (43 percent). The overall frequency of family meals tended to be higher in the GUTS study than in Project EAT, which was partly attributable to the lower age of the participants. As in Project EAT, the younger respondents reported eating more family meals per week than did older respondents: 12 percent of the nine year olds reported eating family meals on none or some days, as compared to 24 percent of the fourteen-year-old respondents. The greater frequency of family meals in the GUTS study may also be due to the mothers' being registered nurses and thus being at higher socioeconomic levels and presumably having greater health awareness.

The GUTS study also found that young people who ate more frequent family meals had healthier diets. They were less likely to consume ready-made meals (such as frozen dinners, canned food, and microwave meals). Those who ate family meals "never" or "some days" reported eating 1.9 ready-made meals in the past week compared to 1.4 ready-made meals among respondents who ate family meals every day. Higher frequency of family meals was also associated with higher consumption of fruits and vegetables. Respondents who ate a family dinner every day consumed an average of 0.8 servings more of fruits and vegetables than those who ate a family dinner never or only on some days. The frequency of family meals was also positively associated with respondents' intake of fiber, folate, calcium, iron, and vitamins B6, B12, C, and E. Frequency of family meals was inversely associated with consumption of saturated and trans fat, soft drinks, and fried foods. No associations were found with whole dairy foods, snack foods, and red and processed meats. Results were not materially changed after adjusting for potential confounders that might reflect an overall healthier home or lifestyle such as age, gender, body mass, physical activity, television watching, active and passive smoking, household income, and presence of two parents in the home. The findings of the GUTS study confirm that family meals have a robust relationship with positive nutritional intake.

Videon and Manning (2003) analyzed data from the National Longitudinal Study of Adolescent Health (the Add Health Study) to examine associations between family meal patterns and adolescent consumption of fruits, vegetables, dairy foods, and breakfast. The study population is a nationally representative sample of adolescents in grades 7 to 12 in the United States. Data for the analysis being discussed here were collected in 1995 from 18,177 adolescents in this age range. Although this study involved less comprehensive measurement of dietary intake than Project EAT and the GUTS study, it had the strength of using a nationally representative sample.

In the Add Health study, adolescents were asked how many times at least one parent was present when they ate their evening meal in the past seven days. Thus, the question focused more on parental presence at dinner than on family meals. Videon and Manning divided respondents into three groups: 31 percent of teens reported eating three or fewer meals that week with a parent, 21 percent reported four or five meals, and 48 percent reported having six to seven meals with a parent in the past seven days. Consumption of fruits, vegetables, and dairy foods was assessed by asking adolescents how frequently they ate foods in these categories the previous day. Responses were dichotomized for each food category; poor consumption was defined as having eaten fewer than two servings of foods in each category the previous day. Adolescents were also asked what they usually ate for breakfast, and a single measure was constructed to indicate whether adolescents ate anything for breakfast.

Findings were consistent with the other two studies. Even while adjusting for body weight perceptions and sociodemographic characteristics, the number of evening meals eaten with a parent present was significantly associated with adolescents' eating patterns. Compared with adolescents who ate three or fewer family meals, adolescents who ate four to five meals with a parent present were 39 percent less likely to skip breakfast, 19 percent less likely to report poor consumption of vegetables, 22 percent less likely to report poor consumption of fruits, and 19 percent less likely to report poor consumption of dairy foods. The beneficial effect of family meals increased as the number of meals increased. Adolescents who ate six to seven family meals were 52 percent less likely to skip breakfast, 38 percent less likely to report poor consumption of vegetables, 31 percent less likely to report poor consumption of fruits, and 27 percent less likely to report poor consumption of dairy foods, than adolescents who ate three or fewer family meals.

The findings of these three large-scale studies all showed strong, positive associations between family meal frequency and quality of dietary intake in teenagers. Eating a greater number of family mealtimes each week was consistently linked with teens' increased intake of fruits and vegetables, vitamins, calcium, and other healthful nutrients. It was also associated with their decreased intake of prepackaged, fried, and other poor-quality foods and drinks. Despite differences across these studies in terms of study populations (ethnicity/race, socioeconomic status, location within the United States, and age), measures used to assess family meal patterns and dietary patterns, and analyses and treatment of data, the findings were strikingly similar.

An unanswered question is what exactly accounts for these relationships. They could result from the increased availability of healthier foods at family meals, increased discussions about the importance of nutrition at family meals, modeling healthy eating patterns, increased structure of eating at home, or a mixture of these factors. Previous research has shown that availability and accessibility of specific foods are likely to influence adolescents' food choices (Neumark-Sztainer et al. 1999; Neumark-Sztainer, Wall, et al., 2003). As one teenage boy told us in our Project EAT focus group discussions, "They [parents] have healthy food on the table so I just eat what they have." It is important to note that the findings in each study remained statistically significant after adjusting not only for sociodemographic characteristics, but for other measures of potential confounders that might reflect a healthier lifestyle or home environment. This suggests that it is family meals themselves, or things that take place at family meals, that influence young people's dietary intake.

Family Meals and Disordered Eating Behaviors

Research suggests that family mealtimes may not only foster healthy eating but may also act as a protective factor against disordered eating behaviors such as unhealthy weight control behaviors and binge eating in adolescents. Given the concern about teens' high prevalence of disordered eating, Project EAT was designed to examine the correlates of these behaviors in an effort to guide the development of more effective programs aimed at their prevention. Previous large studies of adolescents have suggested the role of broad familial factors such as family connectedness in protecting youth from high-risk behaviors (Resnick, Harris, & Blum, 1993; Resnick et al., 1997). Few studies, however, have examined the specific role of family meals in protecting youth from disordered eating, and those that have been done have tended to focus on small, narrowly defined populations such as female college students or girls with diabetes (Ackard & Neumark-Sztainer 2001; Mellin, Neumark-Sztainer, Patterson, & Sockalosky, 2004; Crowther,

Kichler, Sherwood, & Kuhnert, 2002; Miller, McCluskey-Fawcett, & Irving 1993; Worobey, 2002), thus limiting their generalizability and utility for guiding the development of public health interventions. I will summarize our findings from Project EAT and then report findings from another study we did that has implications for health interventions.

In Project EAT, we examined the importance of family meal frequency to adolescents' disordered eating and also the importance of other meal-related factors, such as the priority given to family mealtimes, their atmosphere, and their structure. "Priority" of mealtimes referred to the degree to which families made meals a priority over competing activities. "Atmosphere" referred to respondents' mealtime enjoyment, conversations, and the amount of arguments that occurred during the meal. "Structure" meant the rules that parents imposed around mealtimes and expectations regarding eating around the table, having manners, and eating what is being served.

Based on previous research, we thought that family meals might be protective against disordered eating behaviors in that they provide a venue for modeling healthy eating patterns, connecting with teenagers, monitoring their eating behaviors, and detecting emerging problematic eating behaviors at an early stage of their development. Since family meals might be a proxy measure for overall familial relationships and communication, we adjusted for family connectedness in our analyses to examine the independent role of family meals. We also adjusted for weight-specific pressures within the home, such as parental encouragement of teens to diet and body mass index of teens, since both of these factors could be associated with disordered eating behaviors and family meal participation. As in the other analyses, adjustments were also made for sociodemographic characteristics.

We found that adolescents were less likely to engage in disordered eating behaviors when they reported more frequent family meals, high priority of family meals in their homes, a positive atmosphere at family meals, and a more structured family meal environment (Neumark-Sztainer, Wall, Story, & Fulkerson, 2004). Among girls, strong associations were found between family meal patterns and disordered eating. For example, 9 percent of girls who reported three to four family meals in the past week engaged in extreme weight control behaviors (self-induced vomiting or use of laxatives, diet pills, or diuretics) as compared with 18 percent of girls who reported no family meals in the prior week. Nine percent of girls who reported a very positive atmosphere at family meals engaged in extreme weight control behaviors, as compared to 22 percent of girls who reported a very negative atmosphere. Among boys, family meal patterns were also associated with disordered eating. Four percent of the boys who reported three to four family meals in the past week engaged in extreme weight control behaviors, as compared with 9 percent of the boys who reported no family meals. Two percent of boys who reported a very positive atmosphere at family meals engaged in extreme

NEW DIRECTIONS FOR CHILD AND ADOLESCENT DEVELOPMENT • DOI 10.1002/cad

weight control behaviors, as compared with 9 percent of boys who reported a very negative atmosphere at family meals.

These associations between family meals and disordered eating were somewhat weakened after adjusting for more global familial factors, such as family connectedness and weight-specific pressures within the home. Nonetheless, a number of the associations remained statistically significant, suggesting an independent relationship between family meals and disordered eating. For example, even after controlling for the other variables, in comparison to girls who did not eat any family meals in the past week, girls eating three to four family meals were at approximately half the risk for extreme weight control behaviors (odds ratio = 0.52) and girls eating five or more family meals were at about a third the risk (odds ratio = 0.33). Associations between family meal patterns and disordered eating tended to be stronger among girls than among boys, perhaps due to increased sensitivity of girls to familial nuances, different interpretations of the terms *dieting* and *binge eating*, and higher frequencies of disordered eating behaviors in the girls than in the boys.

Findings from Project EAT showing strong associations between family meal patterns and disordered eating patterns are similar to our findings in another study, in which we used a completely different study design and study population. The AHEAD study (Assessing Health and Eating in Adolescents with Diabetes) focused on diabetic teens, a population that faces particularly strong requirements to control their food intake in order to remain healthy. In the AHEAD study, we conducted individual interviews with thirty adolescent girls (ages thirteen to twenty years) with type 1 diabetes mellitus (Mellin et al., 2004; Neumark-Sztainer, Patterson, et al., 2002). We also interviewed their parents in separate interviews. Half of the girls (*n* = 15) had reported disordered eating behaviors or insulin misuse for weight control behaviors in a previously distributed survey to a clinic population, and the other half had not reported any such behaviors and were matched with the index group for age, ethnicity, and body mass index. The interviews were semistructured and lasted between sixty and ninety minutes. The interviews were tape-recorded, transcribed verbatim, and coded for emerging themes using content analysis. We were interested in exploring links between familial factors and unhealthy weight control behaviors in adolescents with diabetes mellitus because of the nature of this condition, which places so much emphasis on controlled food intake and has implications for the entire family.

Findings from AHEAD revealed two major differences between the index and comparison groups. Girls engaging in disordered eating behaviors or insulin misuse, or both, came from families in which family meals were less frequent and less structured and weight was discussed often and in a negative manner. Girls with disordered eating were more than three times as likely to be categorized as having a low level of family structure than families of the comparison girls (67 percent versus 20 percent, respectively). Furthermore, the combination of low family meal structure and high familial weight concern was much more prevalent in families of daughters with disordered eating behaviors (58 percent) than in families of comparison girls (7 percent).

Findings from this study suggest the importance of structured family meals, while avoiding an overemphasis on weight-related issues. The interesting finding in the AHEAD study was that although the interview was broad in its scope, with opportunities for adolescents and their parents to branch off into many different directions, family meals emerged as a very strong protective factor for disordered eating behaviors in this high-risk group of girls.

Summing Things Up: Do Family Meals Make a Difference?

Adolescence is a period of high energy and nutrient needs, yet many adolescents are not eating in accordance with dietary recommendations. Findings from the studies reviewed here show clear positive associations between family meal patterns and the quality of dietary intake in adolescents. Teens who eat more meals with their families show higher intakes of fruits, vegetables, and essential nutrients; lower intakes of less nutritious foods; and appear to be at less risk for experiencing disordered eating behaviors such as binge eating. However, quantity is not the only aspect of family mealtimes that matters for teens; quality counts too. Teens in families that make eating mealtimes together a priority, provide rules and structure to mealtimes, and maintain an enjoyable mealtime atmosphere are less likely to engage in unhealthful eating and dieting behaviors.

Our ability to draw these conclusions is strengthened by the consistency of the findings seen across the three large projects discussed in this chapter. Despite the use of different study populations and measures, these studies all found strong and positive relationships between family meal patterns and teens' quality of dietary intake. The findings are also consistent with other research findings showing the importance of home availability of foods as a predictor of intake. In Project EAT, we found that home availability of fruits and vegetables is the strongest correlate of adolescent intake of fruits and vegetables (Neumark-Sztainer, Wall, et al., 2003).

It should be cautioned that the studies discussed in this chapter share one key limitation: they are all cross-sectional. While it seems more logical to assume that family meals are influencing dietary intake, rather than the reverse, we cannot conclude causality from cross-sectional studies. For example, while more family mealtimes are correlated with less disordered eating among teens, it is possible that this relationship exists because a teenage girl trying to restrict her diet or a teenage boy engaging in binge eating behaviors might be less likely to choose to come to the family dinner table. For this reason, longitudinal studies are needed to better understand the role of family mealtimes in shaping adolescents' eating and dieting behaviors.

Although caution is warranted, several important implications for parents and practitioners can be taken from the research. The findings suggest the importance of striving to increase the frequency of family meals in the homes of teens and improving the atmosphere at family meals. Family members should minimize topics of conversations likely to lead to arguments, such as household chores, homework, and children's diets. Suggestions need to take into account the reality of modern families. The aim should not be to make parents feel guilty about not preparing enough home-cooked meals but rather to explore ways to share food preparation tasks with their teens, find easy ways to make healthy food choices, model healthier eating patterns, and find eating patterns that work for individual families (Neumark-Sztainer, 2005). Families should be made aware of the importance of family meals and encouraged to think about how to make these meals more of a priority in their own homes. Every family needs to explore what might work best for them: dinners every evening, brunch on Sundays, or eating out on Tuesdays without cell phones. Breakfast may be a better option in some families than dinner.

If family meals are to happen on a more regular basis, broader social networks surrounding families need to support family meals. Places of employment may want to limit work obligations of parents around the dinner hour. School and community sports organizations may need to take into account family meal practices of the youth that they serve. Restaurants and food manufacturers may be able to profit from the promotion of healthy family foods to be eaten away from home, picked up on the way home from work, or delivered home ready to heat and serve. Improving the nutrition of our youth needs to become a priority of families and communities in the light of the high number of adolescents who are not meeting dietary recommendations, are overweight, and are engaging in unhealthy weight control behaviors. Research findings clearly suggest that family meals have the potential to make significant contributions to the improvement of adolescents' dietary intakes. Families and broader communities need to be made aware of these findings and consider steps that can be taken to help bring families to the table.

References

Ackard, D., & Neumark-Sztainer, D. (2001). Family mealtime while growing up: Associations with symptoms of bulimia nervosa. *Eating Disorders: The Journal of Treatment and Prevention, 9,* 239–249.

Crowther, J. H., Kichler, J. C., Sherwood, N. E., & Kuhnert, M. E. (2002). The role of familial factors in bulimia nervosa. *Eating Disorders, 10,* 141–151.

Gillman, M. W., Rifas-Shiman, S. L., Frazier, A. L., Rockett, H. R., Camargo Jr., C. A.,

Field, A. E., Berkey, C. S., & Colditz, G. A. (2000). Family dinner and diet quality among older children and adolescents. *Archives of Family Medicine, 9*(3), 235–240.

Lino, M., Gerrior, S. A., Basiotis, P. P., & Anand, R. S. (1998). *A report card on the diet quality of children.* Washington, DC: USDA, Center for Nutrition Policy and Promotion.

Mellin, A. E., Neumark-Sztainer, D., Patterson, J., & Sockalosky, J. (2004). Unhealthy weight management behavior among adolescent girls with type 1 diabetes mellitus: The role of familial eating patterns and weight-related concerns. *Journal of Adolescent Health, 35*(4), 278–289.

Miller, D.A.F., McCluskey-Fawcett, K., & Irving, L. M. (1993). Correlates of bulimia nervosa: Early family mealtime experiences. *Adolescence, 28*(111), 621–635.

Neumark-Sztainer, D. (2005). *"I'm, like, so fat!" Helping your teen make healthy choices about eating and exercise in a weight-obsessed world.* New York: Guilford Press.

Neumark-Sztainer, D., & Hannan, P. J. (2000). Weight-related behaviors among adolescent girls and boys: Results from a national survey. Archives of Pediatrics and *Adolescent Medicine, 154*(6), 569–577.

Neumark-Sztainer, D., Hannan, P. J., Story, M., Croll, J., & Perry, C. (2003). Family meal patterns: Associations with sociodemographic characteristics and improved dietary intake among adolescents. *Journal of the American Dietetic Association, 103*(3), 317–322.

Neumark-Sztainer, D., Patterson, J., Mellin, A., Ackard, D. M., Utter, J., Story, M., & Sockalosky, J. (2002). Weight control practices and disordered eating behaviors among adolescent females and males with type 1 diabetes. *Diabetes Care, 25*(8), 1289–1296.

Neumark-Sztainer, D., Story, M., Ackard, D., Moe, J., & Perry, C. (2000). The "family meal": Views of adolescents. *Journal of Nutrition Education, 32,* 329–334.

Neumark-Sztainer, D., Story, M., Hannan, P. J., & Croll, J. (2002). Overweight status and eating patterns among adolescents: Where do youth stand in comparison to the Healthy People 2010 objectives? *American Journal of Public Health, 92*(5), 844–851.

Neumark-Sztainer, D., Story, M., Hannan, P. J., Perry, C. L., & Irving, L. M. (2002). Weight-related concerns and behaviors among overweight and non-overweight adolescents: Implications for preventing weight-related disorders. *Archives of Pediatrics and Adolescent Medicine, 156*(2), 171–178.

Neumark-Sztainer, D., Story, M., Perry, C., & Casey, M. A. (1999). Factors influencing food choices of adolescents: Findings from focus-group discussions with adolescents. *Journal of the American Dietetic Association, 99*(8), 929–937.

Neumark-Sztainer, D., Wall, M. M., Hannan, P. J., Story, M., Croll, J., & Perry, C. (2003). Correlates of fruit and vegetable intake among adolescents: Findings from Project EAT. *Preventive Medicine, 37*(3), 198–208.

Neumark-Sztainer, D., Wall, M., Story, M., & Fulkerson, J. A. (2004). Are family meal patterns associated with disordered eating behaviors among adolescents? *Journal of Adolescent Health, 35*(5), 350–359.

Resnick, M. D., Bearman, P. S., Blum, R. W., Bauman, K. E., Harris, K. M., Jones, J., Tabor, J., Beuhring, T., Sieving, R. E., Shew, M., Ireland, M., Bearinger, L. H., & Udry, J. R. (1997). Protecting adolescents from harm: Findings from the National Longitudinal Study on Adolescent Health. *Journal of the American Medical Association, 278*(10), 823–832.

Resnick, M. D., Harris, L. J., & Blum, R. W. (1993). The impact of caring and connectedness on adolescent health and well-being. *Journal of Pediatrics and Child Health, 29*(Suppl. 1), S3–S9.

Rockett, H.R.H., Breitenbach, M. A., Frazier, A. L., Witschi, J., Wolf, A. M., Field, A. E., & Colditz, G. A. (1997). Validation of a youth/adolescent food frequency questionnaire. *Preventive Medicine, 26*(6), 808–816.

Rockett, H. R., Wolf, A. M., & Colditz, G. A. (1995). Development and reproducibility of a food frequency questionnaire to assess diets of older children and adolescents. *Journal of the American Dietetic Association, 95*(3), 336–340.

Serdula, M. K., Collins, E., Williamson, D. F., Anda, R. F., Pamuk, E., & Byers, T. E. (1993). Weight control practices of U.S. adolescents and adults. *Annals of Internal Medicine, 119*(7), 667–671.

Story, M., French, S., Resnick, M., & Blum, R. (1995). Ethnic/racial and socioeconomic differences in dieting behaviors and body image perceptions in adolescents. *International Journal of Eating Disorders, 18*(2), 173–179.

Story, M., Holt, K., & Sofka, D. (Eds). (2000). *Bright futures in practice: Nutrition.* Arlington, VA: National Center for Education in Maternal and Child Health.

Videon, T. M., & Manning, C. K. (2003). Influences on adolescent eating patterns: The importance of family meals. *Journal of Adolescent Health, 32,* 365–373.

Worobey, J. (2002). Early family mealtime experiences and eating attitudes in normal weight, underweight and overweight females. *Eating and Weight Disorders, 7,* 39–44.

DIANNE NEUMARK-SZTAINER is a professor in the Division of Epidemiology and Community Health and an adjunct professor in the Division of General Pediatrics and Adolescent Health at the University of Minnesota.

NEW DIRECTIONS FOR CHILD AND ADOLESCENT DEVELOPMENT • DOI 10.1002/cad

INDEX

Back Issue/Subscription Order Form

Copy or detach and send to:

Jossey-Bass, A Wiley Imprint, 989 Market Street, San Francisco CA 94103-1741

Call or fax toll-free: Phone 888-378-2537 6:30AM —3PM PST; Fax 888-481-2665

Back Issues: Please send me the following issues at $29 each

(Important: please include series initials and issue number, such as CD99.)

_____

_____

_____

$ _____ Total for single issues

$ _____ SHIPPING CHARGES: SURFACE   Domestic   Canadian

		Domestic	Canadian
First Item		$5.00	$6.00
Each Add'l Item		$3.00	$1.50

For next-day and second-day delivery rates, call the number listed above.

Subscriptions   Please __ start __ renew my subscription to *New Directions for Child and Adolescent Development* for the year 2 _____ at the following rate:

U.S.	__ Individual $90	__ Institutional $220
Canada	__ Individual $90	__ Institutional $260
All Others	__ Individual $114	__ Institutional $294

$ _____ Total single issues and subscriptions (Add appropriate sales tax for your state for single issue orders. No sales tax for U.S. subscriptions. Canadian residents, add GST for subscriptions and single issues.)

__ Payment enclosed (U.S. check or money order only)

__ VISA __ MC __ AmEx # _____ Exp. Date _____

Signature _____ Day Phone _____

__ Bill Me (U.S. institutional orders only. Purchase order required.)

Purchase order # _____

Federal Tax ID13559302   **GST 89102 8052**

Name _____

Address _____

_____

Phone _____ E-mail _____

For more information about Jossey-Bass, visit our Web site at www.josseybass.com

OTHER TITLES AVAILABLE IN THE
NEW DIRECTIONS FOR CHILD AND ADOLESCENT DEVELOPMENT SERIES
Reed W. Larson and Lene Arnett Jensen, Editors-in-Chief
William Damon, Founding Editor-in-Chief

NEW DIRECTIONS FOR
CHILD AND ADOLESCENT DEVELOPMENT
IS NOW AVAILABLE ONLINE AT WILEY INTERSCIENCE

What is Wiley InterScience?

Wiley InterScience is the dynamic online content service from John Wiley & Sons delivering the full text of over 300 leading scientific, technical, medical, and professional journals, plus major reference works, the acclaimed Current Protocols laboratory manuals, and even the full text of select Wiley print books online.

What are some special features of Wiley InterScience?

Wiley Interscience Alerts is a service that delivers table of contents via e-mail for any journal available on Wiley InterScience as soon as a new issue is published online.

EarlyView is Wiley's exclusive service presenting individual articles online as soon as they are ready, even before the release of the compiled print issue. These articles are complete, peer-reviewed, and citable.

CrossRef is the innovative multi-publisher reference linking system enabling readers to move seamlessly from a reference in a journal article to the cited publication, typically located on a different server and published by a different publisher.

How can I access Wiley InterScience?

Visit http://www.interscience.wiley.com.

Guest Users can browse Wiley InterScience for unrestricted access to journal tables of contents and article abstracts, or use the powerful search engine.

Registered Users are provided with a *Personal Home Page* to store and manage customized alerts, searches, and links to favorite journals and articles. Additionally, Registered Users can view free online sample issues and preview selected material from major reference works.

Licensed Customers are entitled to access full-text journal articles in PDF, with select journals also offering full-text HTML.

How do I become an Authorized User?

Authorized Users are individuals authorized by a paying Customer to have access to the journals in Wiley InterScience. For example, a university that subscribes to Wiley journals is considered to be the Customer.

Faculty, staff and students authorized by the university to have access to those journals in Wiley InterScience are Authorized Users. Users should contact their library for information on which Wiley journals they have access to in Wiley InterScience.

ASK YOUR INSTITUTION ABOUT WILEY INTERSCIENCE TODAY!